D0646230

SUBJECT TO CHANGE
creating great products and services for an uncertain world

adaptive **path**

SUBJECT TO CHANGE
creating great products and services for an uncertain world

Peter Merholz
Brandon Schauer

David Verba
Todd Wilkens

O'REILLY®

BEIJING · CAMBRIDGE · FARNHAM · KÖLN · PARIS · SEBASTOPOL · TAIPEI · TOKYO

Subject to Change:
Creating Great Products and Services for an Uncertain World
by Peter Merholz, Todd Wilkens, Brandon Schauer, David Verba

Copyright © 2008 Adaptive Path. All rights reserved.
Printed in United States of America

Published by O'Reilly Media, Inc. 1005 Gravenstein Highway North,
Sebastopol CA 95472

O'Reilly books may be purchased for educational, business, or sales promotional
use. Online editions are also available for most titles (*safari.oreilly.com*). for more
information, contact our corporate/institutional sales department: (800) 998-9938
or *corporate@oreilly.com*.

Editor: Edie Freedman
Interior Designer: Ron Bilodeau
Illustrator: Robert Romano
Cover Designer: Kumi Akiyoshi

Print History: February 2008, First Edition

The O'Reilly logo is a registered trademark of O'Reilly Media, Inc. The Adaptive Path
logo is a registered trademark of Adaptive Path, LLC

Many of the designations used by manufacturers and sellers to distinguish their
products are clarified as trademarks. Where those designations appear in this book,
and O'Reilly Media, Inc. was aware of a trademark claim, the designations have been
printed in caps or initial caps.

While every precaution has been taken in the preparation of this book, the publishers
and authors assume no responsibility for errors and omissions, or for damages
resulting from the use of the information contained herein.

ISBN-10: 0-596-51683-5
ISBN-13: 978-0-596-51683-3
[M]

Contents

Introduction vii

CHAPTER 1: **The Experience Is the Product** 1

CHAPTER 2: **Experience as Strategy** 15

CHAPTER 3: **New Ways of Understanding People** 35

CHAPTER 4: **Capturing Complexity, Building Empathy** 59

CHAPTER 5: **Stop Designing "Products"** 79

CHAPTER 6: **The Design Competency** 103

CHAPTER 7: **The Agile Approach** 151

CHAPTER 8: **An Uncertain World** 173

Bibliography 179

Index 183

Introduction

Predicting the Future Has Never Been Easy

Throughout most of human history, if you proclaimed your ability to predict the future, people most likely concluded that you were either very wise, endowed with magical powers, or insane. The conclusion they drew depended on your demeanor and their personal world view. If your predictions turned out to be true, you were a hero; if they didn't, you were scorned and shunned. People have always had to choose their predictions carefully.

Sure, some things are easier to predict than others. The tides rise and fall, the seasons come and go. But those aren't the kind of predictions people are most interested in, are they? The predictions that matter are the ones that aren't so easy to make. From the direction of the stock market to the social impact of a new technology, our world is full of complex phenomena whose underlying patterns are difficult to discern.

In response, we've created systems whose chief selling point is their resistance to change. Schools, governments, social structures of all kinds; in a sense, most of what we call "civilization" serves to some degree as a buffer against unexpected change. Without such systems and the stability they provide, it's hard to imagine that the rapid growth and progress of the last 150 years would have been possible.

After all, nowhere is this reliance on predictable systems resistant to change more evident than in the world of business. Companies are always looking for ways to reduce the unpredictability of doing business. They implement operational systems to maximize efficiency. They invest in sales and marketing systems to maintain high levels of customer demand. They search for business models that are impervious to shifts in the competitive landscape.

For creators of products and services, the pressure is particularly acute. The forces of globalization and technological progress have created an environment in which creating a product that isn't obsolete by the time it finds an audience is increasingly difficult. The accelerating pace of change is working against the art of predicting the future.

Predicting the future has never been easy, but it's never been more difficult. As the social and economic environments around us grow ever more complex, the patterns that drive them become subtler and harder to identify. What we need aren't better predictions of the future—because better predictions are proving impossible. Instead, we need a better toolset for responding to the sudden twists and turns the future may have in store.

The book you're reading now is a guide to that toolset.

The key to creating successful products and services in a rapidly changing world is not resistance to unexpected change, but the flexibility to adapt to it. That flexibility must take a number of forms: flexible design processes to adapt to new insights into user behavior, flexible development processes to adapt to new technological opportunities, and flexible decision-making processes to adapt to new competitive and market realities.

The trouble with predictions is that you don't know they're wrong until it's too late. The future is, increasingly, subject to change without notice. The only question is whether to keep seeking new, more accurate predictions, or to seek approaches that will continue to work no matter which prediction comes true.

—Jesse James Garrett
President, Adaptive Path

CHAPTER 1

The Experience Is the Product

How do we deliver great products and services in an uncertain world?
The thing to keep in mind, not just in the abstract, but truly and
viscerally, are your customers and their abilities, needs, and desires.

This is a crucial time for businesses around the world—and we use the word "crucial" intentionally. We're sitting at the crux of a fundamental shift in the ways in which businesses engage with their customers. There are many reasons for this shift—globalization, containerization, digitization—and these emerging forces are causing consternation for businesses that don't quite know how to react. The old tools at their disposal, such as efficiency, optimization, just-in-time manufacturing, blitz marketing, and outsourcing no longer provide the gains or competitive advantages they once did.

The key to succeeding in the contemporary marketplace is to fundamentally change your relationship with customers. Once you stop thinking of your customers as consumers and begin approaching them as people, you'll find a whole new world of opportunities to meet their needs and desires.

Seizing those opportunities is another matter. Businesses must stop thinking of their products and services as standalone offerings, and instead adopt a systems-oriented mindset that better serves people's actual needs. Furthermore, to continually deliver high-quality products, businesses need to incorporate design approaches into their standard work practices and build an internal design competency. This doesn't necessarily mean hiring designers, but at the very least it is critical to understand and appreciate the values and worldview that designers often bring.

Of course, it doesn't end there; you still have to deliver your product or service. Contemporary life is too uncertain for overlong development cycles. By the time a product finally gets released, the world has often moved on. And so businesses need to move away from their onerous technological and engineering approaches, embracing nimbler, more flexible means when building products and services.

In this book, we'll share what we've learned through observing industry trends and conducting our own work at Adaptive Path. But first, we'll tell a story. This is a story about the birth of consumer electronics (although, technically, electricity isn't even a part of the story).

You Press the Button, We Do the Rest

In 1886, *Scientific American* hailed "a new photographic apparatus" (Figure 1-1) as an exemplar of contemporary product design.

Figure 1-1. Engraving of a cutting-edge camera in its day.

Note the complexity of the magazine's description:

> *This apparatus consists of a box containing a camera, A, and a frame, C, containing the desired number of plates, each held in a small frame of black Bristol board. The camera contains a mirror, M, which pivots upon an axis and is maneuvered by the extreme bottom, B. This mirror stops at an angle of 45°, and sends the image coming from the objective to the horizontal plate, D, at the upper part of the camera. The image thus reflected is righted upon this plate.*

As the objective is of short focus, every object situated beyond a distance of three yards from the apparatus is in focus. In exceptional cases, where the operator might be nearer the object to be photographed, the focusing would be done by means of the rack of the objective. The latter can also slide up and down, so that the apparatus need not be inclined when buildings or high trees are being photographed. The door, E, performs the role of a shade. When the apparatus has been fixed upon its tripod and properly directed, all the operator has to do is to close the door, P, and raise the mirror, M, by turning the button, B, and then expose the plate. The sensitized plates are introduced into the apparatus through the door, I, and are always brought automatically to the focus of the objective through the pressure of the springs, R. The shutter of the frame, B, opens through a hook, H, within the pocket, N. After exposure, each plate is lifted by means of the extractor, K, into the pocket, whence it is taken by hand and introduced through a slit, S, behind the springs, R, and the other plates that the frame contains. All these operations are performed in the interior of the pocket, N, through the impermeable, triple fabric of which no light can enter.

An automatic marker shows the number of plates exposed. When the operations are finished, the objective is put back in the interior of the camera, the doors, P and E, are closed, and the pocket is rolled up. The apparatus is thus hermetically closed, and, containing all the accessories, forms one of the most practical of systems for the itinerant photographer.

—La Nature

This passage has something of the quality of a modern-day consumer electronics operating manual. As "the most practical" system for a photographer on the go, doubtless this was on the cutting edge. However, given the complexity of its operation (by reaching the letter "S," the reader must understand 19 separate elements), it's no wonder that, at the time, photography was the province of either professionals or obsessed hobbyists—the geeks of their era.

Then, in 1888, an inventor named George Eastman designed, manufactured, and marketed a camera that forever changed photography, and also consumer products as a whole (Figure 1-2). Eastman had invented a new kind of film four years earlier, roll film, which was much easier to handle than fragile photographic plates. Had Eastman taken a typical engineering approach to designing his roll-film camera, he would have copied the complexity of the camera described above, just on a smaller scale, thus providing an incremental improvement on his predecessors. Instead, he recognized that his roll film could lead to a revolution if he focused on the experience he wanted to deliver, an experience captured in his advertising slogan, "You press the button, we do the rest."

Figure 1-2. The original Kodak camera and a roll of Kodak film.

Thanks to the capabilities of this new film, operating the new camera was extremely simple. Unlike the apparatus described above, the user never needed to open this camera, and there were only three steps to take a picture (Figure 1-3): Pull the Cord (to prepare the shutter); Turn the Key (to advance the film); and Press the Button (to release the shutter). After you'd used 100 exposures, you would send the camera (or just the roll of film) to Eastman, and wait while your pictures were professionally developed and printed for you.

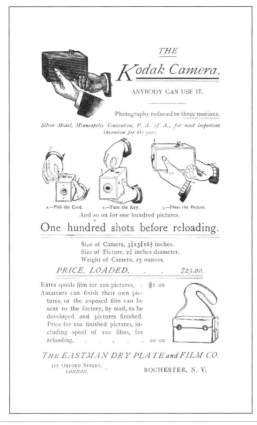

Figure 1-3. An advertisement demonstrates how easy the Kodak is to use.

This level of accessibility began the consumer revolution in photography, and Eastman's camera, the Kodak, became one of the first consumer technology brands. By approaching design with the customer in mind, and not simply as a collection of functional requirements, Eastman arrived at a radically different result.

Increasing the Importance of Design

Throughout the 20th century, businesses largely ignored the lessons from Eastman's experience. Because of the relative simplicity of their offerings, companies felt that an experiential orientation was unnecessary. Products were developed from a technological and feature-based standpoint and, by-and-large, that was fine. An experiential approach to, say, shaving, wouldn't gain you much advantage, and the nature of the tools necessitated a functional approach.

This perspective changed with the rise of computerization, the embedding of microchips in everything—in short, the increasing digitization of our world. Microchips allowed for rapid evolution in product complexity, and product designers, stuck in their old habits, did nothing to allay this. Moore's Law, which states that the number of transistors on a chip doubles every two years, means that those chips packed more and more power, which product designers felt obliged to use.

With instantaneous worldwide digital communication and global shipping streamlined by containerization, the end of the 20th century was a time of even more rapid globalization. Manufacturing costs plummeted as production shifted to Asia. Adding features and functionality wasn't much more expensive, and customers assumed that products that did more things must be better. Today, however, this belief system is reaching a breaking point. Customers now often return items that aren't defective, and in fact work as planned, but turn out to be too complicated to figure out.

As global trends have developed, business management has come to rely on efficiency, optimization, and quality management to deliver value. The good news is that these approaches have worked, and worked well. Many organizations have become very lean, wasting less time, allowing fewer defects, and adopting more efficient processes. Ironically, the bad news is that this type of business optimization is increasingly commonplace. The processes for measuring and controlling efficiency are well-known and well-documented, and so in today's world they no longer provide a significant competitive advantage.

As we plunge deeper into the 21st century, it's becoming clear that companies need to heed George Eastman's lessons. To cut through the complexity of a world that is both shrinking (in terms of the global village) and expanding (with respect to technological capability), businesses must take advantage of the power of design to realize true competitive advantages.

What Do We Mean by Design?

Design is gaining visibility in the world of business. Business reporters proclaim "The Power of Design," as if they've just discovered a secret practice with untold powers. Obviously, design has been around for a while, but it's been saddled with a host of connotations that haven't necessarily served it well:

- **Design as aesthetics**. Perhaps the most commonly held view of design is that it primarily distinguishes a product's aesthetic appeal. Though aesthetics are valuable, this reduction of design to styling alone has limited design's impact in matters that are more than skin deep.

- **Design as a distinct role**. Design is like acting. There are a few gifted naturals, but most designers train long and hard to build the skills and sensitivities to balance form, flow, and function. Therefore, we see designers as professionals who specialize in activities like imagining, drawing, and modeling, which most of us were weaned away from in grade school. Sadly, this discourages non-designers from engaging in design activities to which they might provide a valuable contribution.

- **Design as a thing**. The Museum of Modern Art in New York has a collection dedicated to design, and it features chairs, bowls, typewriters, and salt-and-pepper shakers. Some of the products were financial successes, like the Herman Miller Aeron Chair, and many were not, like Apple's G4 Cube computer (Figure 1-4). This limits the discussion of design as an activity that produces precious artifacts, items that can be placed under glass in a curated display.

- **Design as savior or rock star**. Flip through business magazines or attend a design-related conference and you might start to drink the Kool-Aid. "Design thinking" is "the new black." Design is equated with the equally murky term "innovation." Just design the way Apple does, and success will follow!

Figure 1-4. Even Apple makes mistakes: the G4 Cube was worthy of MOMA, but not the market.

At Adaptive Path, and in this book, we take a different approach to the idea of design. At heart, we believe that design is an activity. As an activity, it incorporates these elements:

- **Empathy**. Design must serve a human purpose, and so design requires an understanding of how people will interact with whatever you're designing.

- **Problem solving**. Design really shines when it's used to address complex problems where the outcome is unclear, many stakeholders are involved, and the boundaries are fuzzy.

- **Ideation and prototyping**. Design produces things, whether they're abstract (schematics, blueprints, wireframes, conceptual models) or concrete (prototypes, physical models). Design is a creative activity, and thus requires actually creating something.

- **Finding alternatives.** Design is less about the analysis of existing options than the creation of new options. Sometimes that means looking at existing options in new ways, and at other times that means creating from scratch. An effective design process typically offers many solutions to a problem.

While there are people who are trained and have deeper experience engaging in these activities, it's far too limiting to consider design the purview of only those called "designers." As we'll discuss throughout this book, for businesses to succeed, design must become an organizational competency.

Technology, Features, Experience

Apple is a company that has parlayed design into phenomenal business success, driven by its CEO, Steve Jobs. Here's what he has said about delivering beautiful solutions:

> *"When you start looking at a problem and it seems really simple, you don't really understand the complexity of the problem. Then you get into the problem, and you see that it's really complicated, and you*

come up with all these convoluted solutions. That's sort of the middle, and that's where most people stop. . . . But the really great person will keep on going and find the key, the underlying principle of the problem—and come up with an elegant, really beautiful solution that works. That's what we wanted to do with Mac."

– Steve Jobs[*]

In that quote, uttered 17 years before the introduction of the iPod and 23 years before the iPhone, Jobs neatly captures the evolution of product offerings. You can strip it down even further to just three key essentials: technology, features, and experience.

Products necessarily begin with the technology that makes them possible. And the introduction of a new technology can establish a company in the market. When VCRs came on the consumer market in the late '70s, all that really mattered is that they did something you could never do before—record television shows so that you could play them back on your own time. It didn't matter that a VCR took up a lot of space and didn't look pretty and wasn't particularly intuitive. It's an example of the walking dog syndrome: a dog doesn't walk very well on its hind legs alone, but we're fascinated and thrilled because it can walk that way at all.

Eventually competitors mimic your technology, and features become the important differentiator. You load your offering with more stuff, and it fills the product's packaging with bullet points. In the 1980s and into the 1990s, VCRs began loading up on functionality by adding VCR Plus, on-screen menus, various playback speeds, child locks, jog wheels, 21-day timers, the ability to record one frame at a time, and more. As Jobs said, "Then you get into the problem, and you see that it's really complicated, and you come up with all these convoluted solutions. That's sort of the middle, and that's

[*] Steven Levy, *Insanely Great: The Life and Times of Macintosh, the Computer That Changed Everything* (Penguin, 2000), p. 139.

where most people stop." It's for this reason the blinking 12:00 became the icon of poorly designed consumer electronics, and most folks used the VCR as simply a videocassette player, viewing whatever they rented.

"But the really great person will keep on going and find the key, the underlying principle of the problem—and come up with an elegant, really beautiful solution that works." At some point, to stay viable, product categories require a quantum evolution that takes them beyond technology and features and on to the satisfaction of a customer experience. The VCR begat the DVR, and TiVo, the leading DVR brand, is successful because the designers began with an experience-focused mindset, and developed the product to fulfill those needs (Figure 1-5).

Figure 1-5. The friendliness and approachability of the TiVo logo demonstrates the company's desire to connect with emotion and experience.

In some ways, it's unfair to compare TiVo with earlier VCRs because the underlying technology is fundamentally different. But, as with George Eastman and his roll film, TiVo took a new technology (hard-drive based, digital video recording) and realized they could change the game if they focused on the customers' experiences. So rather than simply shoving this hard drive inside a VCR, their experience orientation led to a fundamental rethinking of people's relationship to television. And even though TiVo hasn't been the runaway success that its early advocates hoped, this experiential approach has made TiVo the only successful independent DVR after its primary competitor, ReplayTV, went bankrupt.

The Experience Is the Product

We live in an increasingly uncertain world, where the tools that served us well for so long no longer do. Technology isn't sufficient; we can't simply add features to attract an audience. There is no more efficiency to squeeze out of our operations, nor defects to remove from our products.

How do we deliver great products and services in an uncertain world? The thing to keep in mind, not just in the abstract, but truly and viscerally, are your customers and their abilities, needs, and desires. When you do that, when you truly empathize with the people you serve, you'll realize that for them the experience is the product we deliver, and the only thing they truly care about.

CHAPTER 2

Experience as Strategy

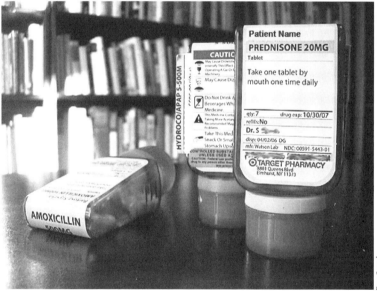

Bart Szyszka

All that matters to customers is their experience.

For decades, businesses have sought technology, features, and optimizations to maintain or increase an advantage over their competitors. But the value of investing solely in these things has reached an end. The experiences people have with your products and services is the real differentiator, a strategy that must be explored and embraced in our changing world.

In the last chapter, we liberally threw the word "experience" around. We even made the claim that "the experience is the product." Now we'll break experience into its component parts, so you see what we mean.

When a person engages with your products, services, and environments, a set of distinctly human qualities comes into play. A person's experience emerges from these qualities:

- **Motivations:** why they are engaged with your offering, and what they hope to get out of it

- **Expectations:** the preconceptions they bring to how something works

- **Perceptions:** the ways in which your offering affects their senses (see, hear, touch, smell, taste)

- **Abilities:** how they are able to cognitively and physically interact with your offering

- **Flow:** how they engage with your offering over time

- **Culture:** the framework of codes (manners, language, rituals), behavioral norms, and systems of belief within which the person operates.

When someone says they've had a good or a bad experience, what they're talking about is how a product, service, or environment did or didn't satisfactorily address these qualities.

Competitive Advantage: A Little History

In the 20th century, in addition to an emphasis on computerization and globalization, business management focused heavily on optimization. The early days of business management began with economic theory and the work of Fredrick Taylor, who performed time and motion studies in factories to scientifically examine and select the most efficient working methods. His approach influenced followers who brought about such commonplace practices as the use of Gantt charts and financial budgeting for accountability. Efficiency became paramount.

Since Taylor, the obsession with optimization has remained constant. An old adage suggests that "you can only manage what you measure," and optimizations and cost-reduction can certainly be measured. If we fast-forward to the latest trends in business management from the past decade, you'll see the same focus on optimization in the popular Six Sigma and Business Process Reengineering (BPR) practices. Six Sigma focuses on quality, attempting to produce only 3.4 defective parts per million "opportunities" to err. With Six Sigma, organizations squeeze costs by searching out and eliminating waste. BPR is a practice of applying similar optimization tactics to business processes (Figure 2-1). A BPR process typically leads businesses to rethink or eliminate activities that don't add significant value.

Take Dell, for example, a company that has so tightly choreographed its supply chain that it can actually sell computers below cost and turn a profit from "float"—the interest made on money between the time they receive a customer's payment for the computer and the time they have to pay the other partners in the supply chain. Now several other manufacturers have emulated Dell's supply chain while also working to differentiate their products, leaving Dell no longer with the lion's share of the market.

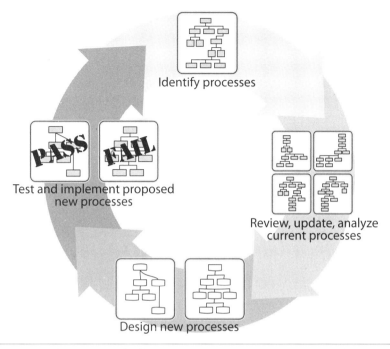

Figure 2-1. The iterative cycle of Business Process Reengineering optimizes what a business already does.

Because techniques of operational efficiency such as Dell's lean, supply-chain management have become increasingly well-known and easily practiced, they're no longer the big competitive advantages they used to be. Aiming to be better at an activity that everyone else has mastered isn't a strategy. Strategy is about tradeoffs—purposefully choosing tactics different than those used by your competition. Strategy means saying no to some activities so you can excel at others. And the result of these strategic tradeoffs is products and services that are clearly distinguished in customers' minds, with meaningful differences that can't easily be replicated by others.

Today, as the benefits of organizational efficiency have decreased, businesses are looking for new approaches to create value for customers and for themselves. The narrow focus on the bottom line—and all the post-profit savings that were created by being efficient—has changed to a focus on the top line, where revenues can be increased by finding new customers and defining new offerings. However, the approaches to finding new and competitive products and services have their own pitfalls.

Escaping Parity

It's the marketing MBA's favorite tool. It gets rolled out at meeting after meeting in all of its analytical, bean-counting glory: the dreaded feature matrix, a document created by some assistant-of-something who compiled a list of all of the companies that might be considered competitors, cataloged all of their products' "features," and tallied the results in a giant matrix.

It's a very logical, thorough approach. By comparing you to your competitors apples-to-apples and oranges-to-oranges, you find where you're ahead, where you're lagging, and where you're absolutely not represented. Unfortunately, the typical response is to focus on the deficient or missing "features." That makes sense: who would want to face the new VP when he's smoldering over the competitor's market-leading Automated Configuration Wizard that you don't even have a response to? The natural response is to seek parity with your competition.

Parity Isn't a Strategy

But what is parity? It's sameness. It's removing differentiation between you and the competition. It's looking only to your competitors for what defines your offering. From your customer's viewpoint, if you've reached parity with your rivals then there's no discernable difference between

---

you and anyone else. The experience can become so banal and impotent that it either ceases to exist, or only the negative aspects of the experience (usability issues, for example) are notable. Avoid the pitfall of parity. Avoid the feature wars, vying to have more bullet points on your packaging and spec sheets than your rivals.

Different is good. Competitive strategy is based on doing things differently than your competitors, and demonstrating the worth of those differences to customers. Seth Godin spent his entire book, *Purple Cow*, explaining the importance and value in developing something different than all of those boring white-and-black Holsteins out there: "Create products and services that are worth marketing in the first place."* Amen. A good experience strategy creates differences that you can present to customers, preserve over time, and perform better than your rivals.

Being the Best Isn't a Strategy

So if reaching parity—being as good as others—is a bad idea, isn't being the best a great idea? Maybe not. Striving to be the best at everything, to be the best in your industry, can be an all too common misstep. The problem with this thinking is that you can't be the best at everything, and besides, being the best depends entirely on who's doing the judging. High school students and affluent baby boomers will have different opinions on whether Taco Bell provides "the best" Mexican restaurant experience.

Instead of just saying you want to be the best, strategy sensei Michael Porter says we should actually be asking, "How can you deliver a unique value to meet an important set of needs for an important set of customers?"† For people who have only 15 minutes to spend

---

* Seth Godin, "In Praise of the Purple Cow," FastCompany.com, January 2003.
† "Michael Porter Asks, and Answers: Why Do Good Managers Set Bad Strategies?" Knowledge@ Wharton, November 1, 2006.

on themselves, Starbuck's delivers a "daily indulgence as coffee break" experience (Figure 2-2). Through a coordinated system that includes a great employment program, thousands of stores, and a carefully curated set of products and environment, Starbucks has a unique feel for the customers who matter to them.

Figure 2-2. Starbucks focuses on providing a predictable and relaxing experience to customers with a few minutes for a break.

The Escape of Novelty

Years ago a national bank began a redesign of its retail customer web site. The bank's business leaders were assured that putting weather information on the customer site would be a big win: everyone likes to know the weather, and none of their competitors had weather information on their sites. They matched a customer need with a unique component to their offering. The only trouble was…the weather has absolutely nothing to do with banking.

Novelty Isn't Differentiation

Weather on a bank site is unique, but that's about all it is. It's just a novelty. Perhaps it's amusing or unusual, but only because it's unexpected. As time wears on, it becomes useless and potentially annoying. Differentiation isn't just about being new, it's also about being relevant.

Yet this is a mistake that organizations make repeatedly, especially with the increasing focus on innovation. A lot of stock is placed in "new." It's easier to make something new than it is to make something that's useful or desirable. Thus many companies pander to novelty at the expense of more beneficial qualities.

Novelty Lacks Context

Crazy predictions peppered the Web prior to the launch of the high-tech Segway scooter (Figure 2-3), aka the "human transporter." Its patented technology was supposed to change cities and create a new world. Steve Jobs referred to it as an "incredibly innovative machine."*

The Segway was certainly new and certainly innovative, but the problem was that no one wanted to use it in the context for which it was intended. Prior to the Segway's launch, both Jobs and Amazon founder Jeff Bezo's shared concerns that they both lived minutes from a grocery store but were unlikely to use a Segway to get there. Why not just walk? The Segway was targeted to fit a need that few, including billionaire CEOs, actually had. The experience of riding on a Segway is new and different, but the Segway technology in its current form isn't relevant to the way people move through their lives.

---

* Steve Kemper, "Steve Jobs and Jeff Bezos meet 'Ginger,'" *Harvard Business School: Working Knowledge*, June 16, 2003.

Figure 2-3. Is the Segway relevant to the way people live their lives?

Why Experience Matters

Strategies of parity are low value and short-lived. Strategies of delivering new offerings for novelty's sake won't survive much further than the infomercial. These approaches center on features and technologies rather than focusing on the one thing that really matters—the experience. But even though experience matters to everyone, we almost always lose sight of it in product development.

No one wants to deliver a product that mystifies its audience. In fact, the inception of most new products is spurred by a need to address an experiential concern. Often though, while creating the product, designers, engineers, product managers, and business analysts get so caught up in the process that they lose sight of the initial goal.

This is a tragedy, because to the customers the experience they have is the only thing that matters. Customers rightfully have little appreciation for the technical workings of a product. Beyond the interface, everything else might as well be magic. Think about a light switch. You flip a switch; a light turns on. How many of us care how it works? Or you put things in the refrigerator, and a day later, when you take them out, they're cold. Magic. You pick up a handset, press seven or ten digits, and are talking to someone far away. Magic.

However, if you take typical product development approaches, you'll see why experience falls by the wayside. Let's say we're writing software. We begin with an idea of a human problem to address, and start making whiteboard sketches of a user interface. As we build it, we become keenly aware of the data that undergirds the application, and the logic that turns that data into something useful. When challenges arise, we typically make decisions at the level of data (we need a different data model; we need to integrate with particular kinds of systems) or logic (getting something to happen is too hard to program, so let's simply throw it out for this release; hey, we've already got a library to make it do something similar, so let's just use that). We make decisions without considering their impact on the experience.

All that matters to customers is their experience. It can be a challenge for product teams to keep that focus in mind, which is why so many teams are derailed by a product's technical details.

Maintaining Experiential Focus

There are a number of ways to encourage and maintain an experiential focus throughout your development process. One way is to hire Steve Jobs as your CEO. Apple's success in delivering satisfying experiences stems directly from Jobs' maniacal focus on customers' interactions with products. As CEO, he ensures that Apple delivers only the best designs. And Jobs acts not only as a designer, but also as the ultimate customer. By designing products to make Steve happy, Apple can deliver a kind of experiential coherence in its products that other companies don't. Unfortunately, Jobs is busy, so he's unlikely to accept any job offers. The upside is that it's not an insurmountable challenge; you can go it on your own.

At Adaptive Path, we believe that a key step to organizational success is through employing what we call an "experience strategy." An experience strategy is a clearly articulated touchstone that influences all of the decisions made about technology, features, and interfaces. Whether in the initial design process or as the product is being developed, such a strategy guides the team and ensures that the customer's perspective is maintained throughout.

All too often, product teams have no central vision to work toward. At best, there is a list of requirements to meet; more typically, they simply have a set of features to develop. Designing and developing to requirement and feature lists leads to unsatisfactory experiences, because those lists aren't oriented to the perspective of the user. As they make decisions along the way, teams' concerns for features, data, and technology trumps serving the customer. This is in large part because they have requirement and feature lists in front of them, but nothing to represent the user's ultimate experience.

This is where experience strategy comes into play. As our colleague Jesse James Garrett has commented, experience strategy serves as "a star to sail your ship by." Experience strategies help your company to start designing from the outside in, i.e., from the perspective of those who will be using the product or service you're providing. It's an overarching plan that starts with the customer and works its way back through to your organization's operations and infrastructure.

An experience strategy can take many forms. At its heart is a vision, an expression of the experience you hope customers will have. The next level up from this concise vision statement is a bulleted list of experience requirements, an approach employed by the product team that built Google Calendar. Online calendars seemed like a saturated field, and calendars mostly served as adjuncts to web mail services. Yahoo, with the most popular email program, also had the most popular calendar; MSN's calendar was number two, thanks to Hotmail. How could Google compete, when Gmail's market share was so much smaller (market share as of May 2006: Yahoo Mail, 42 percent; MSN Hotmail, 23 percent; Gmail, 2.5 percent[*])?

What the Google Calendar team realized was that online calendars had never taken experience into account. There was an opportunity to change the game by moving past technology and features. So Google conducted in-home interviews with a range of people to better understand their behaviors and motivations around calendar use. They realized that a calendar isn't simply a tool, but an anchor point in someone's life, making it a surprisingly emotional subject. Coming out of those interviews, they developed a vision for Google Calendar, articulated from the perspective of how it could satisfy users' experiential needs:

- Fast, visually appealing, and joyous to use
- Drop-dead simple to get information into the calendar

---

[*] Bill Tancer, "Google, Yahoo! and MSN: Property Size-up," Hitwise.com blog, May 19, 2006.

- More than boxes on a screen (reminders, invitations, etc.)
- Easy to share so you can see your whole life in one place

It may not be sexy, but it was effective at keeping a team oriented around a common goal, and the Google Calendar team's experiential approach is proving successful. Yahoo and MSN's offerings had been available for years, but after only eight months, Google Calendar surpassed MSN, coming in a close second to Yahoo (Figure 2-4).[*]

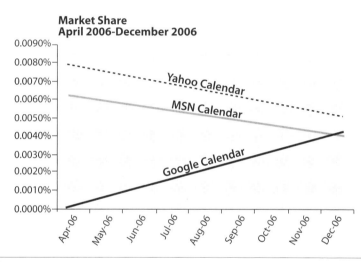

Figure 2-4. Google Calendar's experiential focus guided the service from worst to first.

[*] Leeann Prescott, "Google Calendar Up Threefold Since June," Hitwise.com blog, January 3, 2007.

An Experience Strategy Isn't a Brand Strategy

Some might argue that Google's success is a result of extending its marvelously successful brand. While Google does have remarkable brand awareness, this has had limited impact on their products beyond Search. Yahoo's email, maps, news, and finance products have far larger user numbers than Google's offerings.[*]

Discussions of experience and design inevitably involve brand. The UK Design Council's web site begins its discussion of experience design with this sentence: "Experience design concentrates on moments of engagement between people and brands, and the memories these moments create."[†] But not every organization can be reduced to a brand. Some of the best designing for experience occurs in public institutions—for example, the Seattle Public Library, or the United States Holocaust Memorial Museum. For the people who use them, these places become much more than mere brands.

This brand orientation is antithetical to designing for experience. Traditional brand strategy is practiced as a marketing function; it's about associating a company or its products with a set of values and qualities. Brand begins with the company. As such, it's very much an inside-out orientation: an organization identifies the attributes it wants to project, and does what it can to communicate them to customers.

As marketing consultant Lou Carbone puts it, brand is very much rooted in 19th- and 20th-century practices of "make and sell," of a manufacturing economy that needed to communicate attributes of its products and the companies that made them.[‡]

---

[*] Bill Tancer, ibid.

[†] Ralph Ardill, "Introduction to Experience Design," *http://www.designcouncil.org.uk*, March 26, 2007.

[‡] Lou Carbone, Presentation at Adaptive Path's Managing Experience Conference, February 12, 2007.

Such an approach is insufficient as we shift from "make and sell" to the delivery of services, where products aren't interesting in and of themselves, but only as interfaces to larger systems. In contrast to traditional brand strategy, experience strategy begins with the customer. It's about contributing to a desirable experience, helping people accomplish what they want to get done. Experience comes from the outside in; an appreciation of customers' motivations, behaviors, and context leads to the development of a product, service, or system that can satisfy them.

Adaptive Path recently did a project that highlights the difference. Working with a financial services firm, we were given a set of "brand image attributes" that reflected the company's desired brand, or image:

- Approachable
- Authentic
- Proactive
- Creative
- Knowledgeable
- Vast

However, when observing this company's customers, we realized that the nature of their desired experience had these attributes:

- A simple view of my finances
- Service orientation; receive support and assistance
- Performance assessment; make tracking financial performance easy
- Support basic, day-to-day activities

The first list provides the list of attributes meant to encourage customers to do business. It comprises the "personality" of the company, and we mean that literally—it's an attempt to give the company the attributes of a person. However, that list says nothing about how people want to do business with the company. It simply says what the company wants to project.

That first list was insufficient for moving the company forward. The list of experience attributes guided our efforts in evolving the company's delivery of services, so customers would get what they needed and come away satisfied.

Now, we don't mean to downplay the importance of brand or the role it plays in customer decisions, but it's essential to recognize the traditional practice of brand for what it is—the impression a company tries to make about its personality. People's experience with a product will definitely influence their perception of the brand: Google and TiVo are obvious examples of companies that have done relatively little to impress a brand on the public, but have strong and (mostly) positive brand perceptions.

Embodied Experience Strategy

While an experience strategy can sometimes simply be presented as a list of bullet points, cut-and-dried presentation methods don't bring the strategy to life. Embodying the experience strategy in some kind of prototype can be incredibly effective. A recent example often mentioned in the press involves Deborah Adler's master's thesis in design school. Looking for a suitable subject, she found out that her grandmother had taken her grandfather's medication by mistake. She realized that such mix-ups were too easy. Prescription bottles used haphazard typefaces on labels affixed to curved surfaces that were hard to read. At first glance, all bottles from the same pharmacy look the same. Research showed Deborah that 60 percent of people taking prescriptions had committed errors similar to her grandmother.

Her thesis project, named SafeRX, reconceptualized the pharmacy bottle, incorporating modern typefaces, visual hierarchy, color-coding, and improved bottle design. She shopped it around after graduation, and found an interested suitor in Target. Working with an industrial designer, they turned her initial concepts into ClearRX (Figure 2-5). Her initial SafeRX design served as a prototype experience strategy, a guiding light for all of the people developing the systems that would make it work. When changes were necessary, it was always with an eye to how to maintain the essential qualities of experience. For instance, Adler's initial concept involved color-coding the labels to distinguish each family member's medication. When color printing proved too costly, the experiential quality was delivered through colored rings affixed to the bottle's neck.

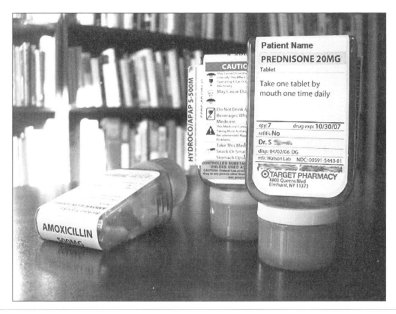

Figure 2-5. The Target ClearRX pill bottle, with many of the components demonstrated in the prototype.

Experience strategy prototypes can also be simplified to the extreme. Product designer Jeff Hawkins measured the sizes of his colleagues' shirt pockets, and then carved a block of wood that would fit inside. He was developing a personal digital assistant, and he knew it was paramount that the device be small enough for easy carrying.*

He carried that block of wood everywhere, and when someone mentioned a date or a piece of information he wanted to jot down, he would mime inputting that information into the block of wood. When his engineers suggested new features and functionality to him, he'd hold up the block of wood and ask, "Where would it go?" The block of wood enforced simplicity in the design and development of the device, continually reminding the team of that tactile experience.

Guided by such an experiential focus, the ensuing device, the PalmPilot, succeeded where others, such as Apple's Newton, had failed (Figure 2-6).

Figure 2-6. The Apple Newton crammed features and promises into its large form-factor; the PalmPilot delivered only the essentials that users needed.

---

* David S. Jackson, "Palm-To-Palm Combat," *Time Magazine*, March 16, 1998.

Creating Effective Experience Strategies

Having an experience strategy means having a strong plan for the experiences your firm offers—a plan so strong that it guides decisions about how the firm executes, maintains, and manages these experiences to create value both for the customers and (as a byproduct) for the firm.

These planned experiences:

- **Truly differentiate themselves** from the perspective of the customer, connecting to something distinct about your firm; feature parity isn't an experience strategy.

- **Are what matter most to customers**—to truly understand these experiences, you have to understand them from the context of the customer. The experiences are what they choose to engage in, not the nuts and bolts that create them.

- **Should be invested in and managed** just as you would manage any other portfolio of opportunities. Business decisions should be made with consideration of the impact on experience.

- **Can be cultivated and nurtured,** while keeping in mind that they arise not from an controlled expression of what the firm says it stands for, but from the customer's perception of the set of distinctly human qualities outlined at the beginning of this chapter.

As you have noticed, much of an experience strategy hinges upon how people perceive experiences.

Understanding the strategic value of listening to the customer's perspective is just the beginning. Practicing experience strategy successfully requires mastery of the topic covered in the next chapter: ways of understanding people.

CHAPTER 3

New Ways of Understanding People

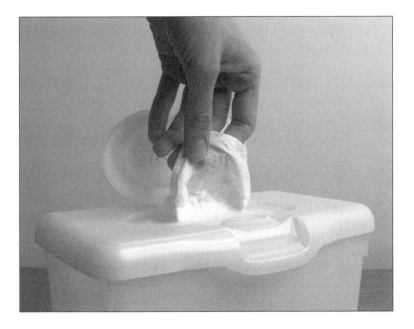

We must understand people as they are rather than as market segments or demographics.

A few years ago, two of Adaptive Path's practitioners worked together as members of a small design team at a company called Epinions.com. Epinions, which has since been acquired by eBay, featured reviews of products and services written by consumers. Reviewers earned money for their reviews, consumers rated those reviews, and other sites syndicated the content. As a whole, the site focused on building a community of authors, raters, and readers, and it was one of the earliest pieces of explicitly "social software," long before services like Friendster, MySpace, or Flickr even existed.

It was a place where the traditional models of understanding people simply as individuals interacting with computers and the traditional business models related to products broke down fairly quickly. Because Epinions was so dependent on community, it had to function as a service and a system rather than simply as a product or site.

At Epinions.com, our customer research began with standard usability practices, where participants came into our lab and performed predetermined tasks with our site and those of our competitors. We quickly realized that we needed to abandon these overly structured methods in favor of research approaches that were more qualitative and contextual. One of our most useful sessions occurred when a woman came into our lab and brought her infant with her. The baby needed some attention at a number of points throughout the session, and it was amazingly instructive to see how the woman dropped in and out of a process that we had always considered to be continuous. Through our conversations with her and others, we began to realize that the process of researching product purchases was generally long and disjointed. We needed to support this process explicitly, and make it easy for people to step away and quickly regain a sense of where they were when they left off.

But the woman with her baby gave us something even more important than insight into processes. Seeing her struggle to use the system one-handed and with continuous interruptions gave us empathy for her that informed our design work throughout the Epinions system. Empathy gave us a flexible and extensible understanding of our users that went far beyond the explicit problems, goals, and tasks associated with the particular situation we were studying. We nurtured and expanded this empathy, using a form of digital ethnography which involved hanging out with and taking part in the online community of reviewers, raters, and readers. This proved to be one of our most effective tools for truly understanding the needs and motivations of the people who used the Epinions system.

As it happened, every member of the company was encouraged (in fact, almost required) to write at least one review and become a part of that community. Perhaps more than anything else, this ensured that understanding wasn't localized in our small design and research team. This participation and observation helped the company as a whole develop a real empathy for the people using the system. That empathy was invaluable when the design and research team was working with sales, marketing, development, product management, and customer service. It eased the burden of communication and translation between different groups and disciplines, which meant that we could spend more time doing and less time communicating.

These experiences are what first made us aware of how much we needed to change our understanding of people, as well as how best to go about gaining that understanding. We began to see that we needed a way of understanding our customers that went beyond classic lab-based usability and human factors. We saw that building an honest empathy with our customers did more for our ability to provide a great service than weeks of usability tests. We also learned that it shouldn't just be up to the research and design team to understand customers, but the organization as a whole. Over the years, these insights have proven themselves over and over through a variety of projects that Adaptive Path has tackled for companies in different industries. We've expanded and refined our understanding of these concepts through that work. In this chapter, we'll share what we've learned.

Empathy

We'll be talking a lot about empathy in design throughout this book; it can be a tricky concept, so it's worth taking some time to discuss it explicitly. To paraphrase a number of dictionaries, empathy is being aware of, sensitive to, and vicariously experiencing the feelings, thoughts, and experience of another without having those feelings, thoughts, or experiences explicitly communicated to you. When you begin to unpack that definition, you see why it's such an effective tool in the hands of an organization trying to provide compelling customer experiences.

When you're designing a product or service, it's crucial to differentiate between empathy and sympathy. Sympathy has two common uses, neither of which is appropriate in design. In the first sense, sympathy means something akin to pity. This maintains a distance between you and the other person or group and doesn't necessitate respect. In fact, it can establish a sense of superiority, especially if your team begins to feel actual pity. The other sense of sympathy is an actual shared experience or feeling, as in people whose situations are nearly identical. This form of sympathy removes objectivity, creating a situation where you would say that a person is "too close" to a problem or situation.

By contrast, empathy is an understanding of a person or group's subjective experience by sharing that experience vicariously. Sharing an experience avoids the distance of pity while vicariousness maintains an observer's level of objectivity. Thus, we could say that empathy is something like a *balanced* curiosity that can lead to a deeper understanding of another person.

Empathy becomes meaningful for organizations when it helps us deal with the uncertainty of human behavior and motivation, by letting us bypass the need to explicitly codify every activity and driver. Empathy takes advantage of our innate human ability to understand things about others, and it goes beyond what they (or even we) can articulate. Everyone knows that effective intuition is an important factor of success in almost every field. You develop your sense of intuition by doing the job, by being in the thick of an activity. Over time, you find yourself able to make quick and accurate decisions based on knowledge that is difficult to explain.

Empathy gives us this kind of ability when it comes to designing and developing services and systems. As the products and services we create become ever more complex and intertwined, we cannot possibly explore all of the contexts and situations in which our customers may find themselves. Even if we could, a catalog of observed behaviors isn't sufficient to craft cohesive and compelling experiences. We need to develop an intuitive understanding of the motivations behind these behaviors. Finding empathy helps us grasp the mechanisms that drive behavior, as opposed to just the observed external actions.

Of course, this raises the question: how do you know if you and your organization have developed empathy for your customers? Building honest empathy in an organization is about much more than intuition or "gut feelings." There are systematic approaches that explicitly challenge intuitive understanding. This is the reason we do research in the first place. Empathic understanding must be balanced by objectively observed behaviors and explanations. If intuition were enough, we'd have no reason to talk to people via surveys, focus groups, interviews, or ethnographies. We'll talk about how to put these ideas into practice in Chapter 4.

And the power of empathy isn't limited to the world of design. Empathy is an especially powerful tool in the hands not only of designers and engineers but also executives, business analysts, marketers, and customer service representatives. Articles on the importance of empathy and holistic understanding of customers can now be found in such corporate mainstays as the *Harvard Business Review*[*] and *BusinessWeek*.[†] Cultivated empathy can be extremely powerful and can have profound effects on organizations.

An example from Adaptive Path's work helps illustrate these concepts. Adaptive Path worked on a project for the interactive arm of a news corporation, let's call it NewsCo, where we saw the real power of empathy when it takes root in an organization. Throughout the project, we dealt with a persistent problem: the management team of NewsCo, who had been working in news for many years, felt that they intuitively understood the needs of their audience quite well. After all, they were news consumers in their professional and personal lives—news "junkies," in fact. They tended to make design decisions using themselves as models. They felt no need to test or expand this understanding through research. And yet, even if they were relatively good at understanding "news junkies," that group constituted only a small part of their actual audience. For the other segments of the audience, the NewsCo management augmented their personal understanding with statistics about news consumption and customer demographics. There was no attempt to actually talk to customers, much less vicariously share their experiences.

After a good deal of convincing on our part, we arranged to conduct a number of interviews and in-home sessions with a variety of NewsCo's customers. We brought members of NewsCo out into the field with us and worked with them to analyze our research findings. We worked hard to demonstrate the value of our approaches as a way of understanding their customers, and to also ensure that this understanding was incorporated into the design work. In the end, we helped NewsCo bring about a significant redesign of the system.

---

[*] Paul Hemp, "My Week as a Room-Service Waiter at the Ritz," *Harvard Business Review*, June 2002, and more.

[†] "Marketers Take a Close Look at Your Daily Routines," *USA Today*, April 29, 2007.

But it was only on a visit to corporate headquarters for a follow-up project that we became aware of an important unintended consequence of the initial research and design work. Involving management and non-researchers in the research process—versus communicating our findings via the standard report—brought about a larger organizational change. We found that some of those same managers with whom we had struggled early in the project had changed their approach to understanding customers. They had begun to see the importance of going beyond statistics or extrapolation from their own behaviors. In fact, their change in perspective was so profound that they marked it publicly by passing out t-shirts that said, "We are not the target audience" (Figure 3-1).

Figure 3-1. A shirt marks an epiphany for NewsCo.

What we see here is an organization developing empathy for its customers. But we also see that empathy isn't an innate ability that some people have and others don't. It can be developed and cultivated through practice, and there are concrete approaches that organizations can use to do that. Creating honest empathy transformed the way NewsCo approached a part of its business. The resulting redesign of their site was a dramatic improvement that received high praise from both their users and the press.

Specifically addressing empathy reveals what has always been at the heart of good human-centered design. Even a little empathy can go a long way in the hands of talented designers, but, for the most part, empathy has been a subtle and implicit aspect of successful design and business. As we'll discuss further, this means that more traditional research approaches and user models haven't been ideal for helping us explicitly develop empathy.

To cultivate empathy for customers and users, it's vital that an organization have a realistic view of those people's lives. We must understand people as they are rather than as market segments or demographics. Before we delve into how you can do that, let's look at some of the less effective ways that organizations have tried to understand their customers. Seeing where others have failed and succeeded will help clarify how you can evolve your company's practices to better understand the people you're trying to serve.

Old Models and Their Problems

As important as customers are to every business, it's amazing how seldom organizations explicitly consider how they think about the people who keep them in business. What we're talking about here are the frameworks that guide organizations in characterizing what their customers are doing and why. Sometimes an organization may not even be conscious of these processes, but models exist nonetheless. Historically, businesses have seen people as consumers, message receivers, rational actors, and human factors. As we'll see, none of these models are sufficient for developing empathy, understanding experience, or dealing with the unpredictability of the human world.

Consumers, Literally

Perhaps the worst model we've come across is one that views people as nothing more than consumers, i.e., purely as a means to make profit. The authors of *The Cluetrain Manifesto* give one of the best accounts of this model and its consequences. With the advent of the industrial age, "the customers who once looked you in the eye while hefting your wares in the market were transformed into consumers."[*] They quote Jerry Michalski, a long-time Internet industry analyst and organizational consultant, who notes that businesses began to see a consumer as really no more than "a gullet whose only purpose in life is to gulp products and crap cash." If you're reading this book, it's unlikely that you or your company take this view, but we're sure you've come across companies that do. This model is not only disrespectful, but it also creates an explicit barrier to developing empathy for your customers and users. It also tells us nothing about the nature of our customers, or the characteristics of the products and services we're creating for them.

Sheep

The change from customers into consumers was accompanied by a serious change in the balance of power in the market. As our *Cluetrain* friends put it, "power swung so decisively to the supply side that 'market' became a verb: something you do to customers." This is the reality we live today. For better or worse, "market" is now used largely as a verb.

---

[*] Christopher Locke, Rick Levine, Doc Searls, and David Weinberger, *The Cluetrain Manifesto: The End of Business as Usual* (Perseus Books Group, 2001), p. 78.

For the most part, marketing refers to the practice of crafting and delivering messages about products, services, and organizations. In the marketing world, customers are seen essentially as sheep: docile and gullible beings drifting here and there according to the prevailing winds of popular opinion and marketing messages (Figure 3-2). This view of people has spawned millions of focus groups and market surveys, as well as an obsession with tracking or trying to influence preference through positioning, packaging, and advertising.

Figure 3-2. How marketers often view customers: as sheep.

The way an organization thinks about the people it hopes to serve can color the outcome of even the most well-meaning company's research and design methods. For example, beginning in the 1930s and 1940s, a number of marketing firms worked diligently to bring social science techniques to bear on product development and marketing products. Many of these approaches are the same methods that we use regularly at Adaptive Path, which we advocate in Chapter 4. But because these organizations and their clients based their approach on the "sheep" model of customers, the insights they gained were focused primarily on persuasion through marketing communication. Companies simply wanted to create and control consumer demand. This worked for a while, but it has become less and less effective over time. A general increase in education and the connectedness of society has led people to become much more savvy about marketing messages. In other words, your current and potential customers are people who are uninterested in your marketing messages and are increasingly empowered to ignore or even subvert them.

The "sheep" view of people has also influenced where organizations focus their energy and resources. In the long run, it has encouraged a major disconnect between marketing and design within many organizations. Thus, we see organizations crafting the story of a product in isolation from the actual creation of that product. This disconnect has led to customers buying products and services only to be disappointed that their experiences don't match the stories they've been told. This, combined with the increase in customer savviness and connection, means that the pendulum of market power has begun to swing back to the demand side. We'll talk about these trends more later, but it's worth noting that these factors help explain the recent proliferation of books that advocate the importance of honesty and authenticity in marketing and product development, such as *The Cluetrain Manifesto,* mentioned above, and *All Marketers Are Liars: The Power of Telling Authentic Stories in a Low-Trust World* by Seth Godin.

The first and foremost problem with the "sheep" view is that it's also disrespectful of the people organizations are ostensibly trying to serve. As with the view that customers are nothing but consumers, this disrespect works directly against building honest empathy.

Homo Economicus

Modern business practices, particularly those taught in most business schools, are based on models from the field of economics. Therefore, many businesses approach people the same way economists do. Economics, for much of its formal history, has used a model of people as "homo economicus" or "rational actors." In this view, human behavior is the result of consciously calculated decisions meant to "maximize utility," i.e., get the most utility for the least effort or expenditure. "Utility" is typically defined as a relative amount of *happiness* or *satisfaction*, but, unfortunately, those two terms are generally not clearly defined. In practice, "utility" is used to reference things like return on investment (ROI), number of features, or number of units, which can be measured quantitatively. The concept of rational actors suggests that we're all highly analytic beings consciously calculating the ROI of our time or money. It assumes a world filled with logical Vulcans from *Star Trek*, or perpetual bookkeepers, obsessively tallying the debits and credits of the relative happiness or satisfaction gained from a given decision.

A distinct advantage of this model of people is that it tends to move organizations beyond a focus on messaging toward the actual aspects or features of products and services. However, it keeps them focused on what prompts the customer's decision to buy rather than on the use or experience provided. In short, these businesses focus on quantity over quality. Remember the evolution of VCRs in Chapter 1? The original VCR had basic recording and playback functions. Later models became so feature-rich as to be almost sentient, yet they're notoriously unusable.

Or consider the wave of internet-enabled blenders, toasters, and refrigerators that appeared and quickly disappeared from the market in the late 1990s. These companies no doubt worked diligently to get Internet connectivity into their products because it added an additional "desirable" feature. In the long run, it was nearly impossible to make these products truly useful or successful because kitchen appliances just aren't the right entryway to the Internet. (For another example of this type of erroneous thinking, see the story of KeyboardCo in Chapter 5.)

The "Human Factor"

What was missing from earlier models of customers was a respectful focus on humans and the way they actually *use* products and services. Where the "homo economicus" model focused us on results by suggesting that people rationalize return, a "tasks and goals" view focuses us on the processes by which people act.

There are two significant occurrences in the last century that helped to establish this new view. The first is the emergence of the field of "human factors" in the early part of the 20th century. This field was the first established approach to design and development that explicitly addressed the people who interacted with products and systems. "Human factors" is named as such because it was an adaptation and extension of the classic "systems design" approach, where there are technological factors and human factors. Humans were seen as explicit components of a system with inputs, outputs, strengths, and limitations. This laid the groundwork for the second significant occurrence: in the middle of the 20th century, the rapid rise of cognitive science established the basic mental model that has since become the shared basis for nearly all of the human-centered design and engineering disciplines, including human factors, ergonomics, usability, human-computer interaction (HCI), and user-centered design. The focus is on tasks and goals; this approach has allowed organizations to model people and their interaction with products and services. This, in turn, has led to great improvements in the functionality and usability of these offerings.

While this approach is an improvement over previous models, it still poses some serious problems. Consider the fundamental premise: people are primarily goal-driven and task-oriented. In other words, people know exactly what they're trying to do and use a set of relatively discrete steps to accomplish this goal. This view assumes a world full of robot-like customers, interfaced to the system and relentlessly pursuing goals, step by step. Or at best, it's a world of Type-A personalities obsessed with optimizing their activities, seeking ever more efficient ways to accomplish their goals.

This "tasks and goals" view leads companies to focus primarily on improving the efficiency and usability of their offerings, which isn't bad in and of itself. It's easy to see how this approach has worked well with the focus on optimization that has been driving so many businesses since the onset of Taylorism (as we discussed in Chapter 2). It's clear from the examples of feature-rich but unusable products (i.e., the VCR) that there is an explicit need to address the usability of products. "Usable" is actually the bare minimum of what a product or service should be; passable, but by no means excellent. The point is that the classic "tasks and goals" viewpoint is too low-level to address all aspects of customer experience. Put another way, you can only get so far by streamlining the shopping cart on your web site.

Not All Wrong, Not Really Right

Now, the "sheep," "homo economicus," and "tasks and goals" models are all idealized approaches, which few organizations adopt in pure form. To be fair, these models aren't strictly wrong—there is some truth and value in each of them. Organizations have seen some measures of success by using them, which explains their longevity. People *do* make rational decisions and want more features for less. People *do* have goals and perform tasks to reach them. People *can* be touched by the right story. But these models are incomplete and are quickly reaching their limit of usefulness.

The fatal flaw of all of these models is that they oversimplify your customers' lives. They reduce complexity in an attempt to deal in a general fashion with the inherent uncertainty of markets and the social world. However, ignoring a problem is not a strategy for long-term success.

Let's face it—the human world is increasingly complex. We're in the midst of a societal shift that is affecting nearly every aspect of our lives. Manuel Castells, a pre-eminent sociologist, describes this shift in his book, *The Rise of the Network Society*. Castells' research is based on social and economic data from a vast array of global sources, and it shows how information technology is fundamentally altering the way we live, and profoundly changing how we conduct business and interact with our customers. As customers become more connected as well as more savvy about technology and media, they gain more power in the marketplace. Businesses have less control, which increases uncertainty and risk. To survive in this sort of environment, organizations need to understand their customers as they really are, now more than ever. For most organizations, this will mean evolving their approaches to address components that have been missing in previous models.

What's Been Missing?

Think about your own life and the lives of people you know. Our relationships are complicated and convoluted; our behaviors can be quirky and erratic. Sometimes we act as individuals, sometimes as groups, sometimes as both at the same time. In short, people's lives are messy. It is quite difficult to capture or describe this complexity in terms of consumption, messaging, rationality, utility, or even tasks and goals. The relationships we have with products and services are no less complex.

For example, Proctor & Gamble created Old Spice High Endurance Hair & Body Wash as part of the company's Old Spice line of products. This new product combined shampoo and body wash, and it was a direct result of research that revealed the blurred boundaries of people's everyday lives. After collecting hours of videotape documenting the showering habits of sample male customers, Proctor & Gamble came to understand something very important and interesting about the way that many men approach getting themselves clean. "We kept seeing men using body wash on their hair."[*]

When we're trying to understand our "users" and "customers," we have to remember that they're people just like us, and just like us they regularly cross understood boundaries and categories. They mix and match products to serve previously unidentified needs, and they have motivations and passions that can't be reduced to utilitarian goals. People are inconsistent, often inarticulate, and they challenge social and cultural boundaries in unexpected ways.

The first step to understanding people is to view them realistically. Accepting our inherent messiness means addressing three elements that the "sheep," "homo economicus," and "tasks and goals" models lack: emotion, culture, and context.

Emotion

Most successful organizations are already aware of the importance of emotion. Marketing and design professionals have always talked about emotions, but research has generally failed to address them in any fundamental way. The closest they usually come is in measuring preference for one product or concept over another. But in recent years this has begun to change. Now, even staunch proponents of cognitive science, which pioneered the "tasks and goals" view of people, are coming around to the importance of emotion and affect. In fact, Don Norman, perhaps the most famous cognitive scientist in the world of design, has dedicated a whole book to the subject.

Norman's book, *Emotional Design,* is especially interesting because it makes the case for understanding customers the way we understand ourselves. Norman starts the book by giving two reasons for his change

---

[*] "Marketers Take a Close Look at Your Daily Routines," *USA Today,* April 29, 2007.

of heart regarding the importance of emotion, one professional and one personal. His official, professional reason for changing his mind is "because of new scientific advances in our understanding of the brain and of how emotion and cognition are thoroughly intertwined. We scientists now understand how important emotion is to everyday life, how valuable. Sure, utility and usability are important, but without fun and pleasure, joy and excitement, and yes, anxiety and anger, fear and rage, our lives would be incomplete."[*]

He also had a personal "Aha!" moment. Like most other cognitive scientists, he believed that emotion was of little importance in explaining human activity and behavior. Thus, when color computer monitors first became widely available, he assumed that they were merely an aesthetic addition but unimportant to the tasks and goals of actual work. But when he experimented with the color monitor, he realized it offered a different kind of benefit.

> *"I borrowed a color monitor to see what all the fuss was about. I was soon convinced that my original assessment had been correct: color added no discernible value for everyday work. Yet I refused to give up the color display. My reasoning told me that color was unimportant, but my emotional reaction told me otherwise."[†]*

Though this "Aha!" moment clearly occurred in the early 1980s, apparently Norman wasn't willing to trust his own experience and intuition until the field of cognitive science was able to provide him with theoretical backup some 15 to 20 years later.

---

[*] Don Norman, *Emotional Design: Why We Love (or Hate) Everyday Things*, (Basic Books, 2005), p. 8.

[†] Norman, *Emotional Design*, p. 9.

Culture and Context

It's no great surprise that humans invest nearly all of their experiences with meaning. From the first kiss to a favorite pair of shoes, our lives are full of stories and significance. People also use products and services differently, depending on where they are and with whom. Yet, for the most part, these things have been given little "official" attention by science (outside of anthropology) or by business (outside of marketing and advertising messages). This is changing. Over the last 30 years, we've seen a steady rise in the importance of culture, meaning, and context in nearly every discipline of social science. For example, *Habits of the Heart*, by Robert Bellah and colleagues, was a scholarly success in sociology and political science as well as a national bestseller. It showed us that successful democratic institutions rely on the attitudes and values of our society as much as its laws and structures. Or consider the cultural turn in psychology that occurred in the 1980s and 1990s. Cultural psychology has shown that "cultural traditions and social practices regulate, express, and transform the human psyche, resulting less in psychic unity for humankind than in ethnic divergences in mind, self, and emotion."[*] These revelations have great repercussions for how we think about design and business.

Along with this cultural turn in academics, we've also seen a growing acceptance of culture and context as important concepts in business and design. Of course, businesses have been dealing with cross-cultural issues for some time, but this has primarily focused on things like internationalization or expanding to new markets. Now an understanding of culture and context is becoming even more vital to business success, as well as a more explicit part of the design process, regardless of where the product or service is being provided. Taking these contextual and cultural aspects into account can greatly improve the final designs of products and services.

---

[*] Shweder, Richard, "Thinking Through Cultures: Expeditions in Cultural Psychology" (Harvard University Press, 1991), p. 72.

For example, Kimberly-Clark conducted field research in the homes of families that led to a redesign of two of their Huggies products (Figure 3-3). Researchers saw that mothers were struggling to hold babies while diapering and bathing them. It became clear that many parents needed to keep one hand on their babies to keep them safe or at least in one place while doing these other things. These insights led to the redesign of both their Huggies Baby Wipes Travel Packs and Huggies Baby Wash, to accommodate one-handed dispensing.* Without understanding the context of how customers were using the products, neither of these designs would have come into being.

This is actually part of a growing trend among all sorts of businesses. Consider the following information from an article in *USA Today*:

> *"Twenty years ago, Microsoft had two researchers who specialized in observing consumers at home or at work. Today, the company has 300.*
>
> *At General Mills, about half the consumer research now involves observing people individually, compared with 10 years ago when about 80 percent of its research was done in focus groups.*
>
> *Procter & Gamble has increased spending on such personal research fivefold since 2000. It spent $200 million in consumer-focused research last year.*
>
> *'We're spending far more time living with consumers in their homes, shopping with them in stores and being part of their lives,' says a P&G executive. 'This leads to much richer insights.'"†*

All of these companies have recognized the importance of getting a more realistic understanding of their customers.

---

* *USA Today*, ibid.
† *USA Today*, ibid.

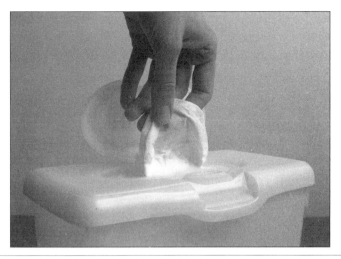

Figure 3-3. Kimberly-Clark redesigned this dispenser after field research revealed that parents often don't have two hands free to get a diaper wipe.

A New Model

Taking emotion, culture, context, and the rest of the messy complexity of human life into account leads us to a new model for understanding our customers. In Chapter 1, we discussed how companies have been evolving the way they approach the design of their products and services. Organizations often begin with a focus on technology, which later becomes a focus on features, and finally develops into a more holistic focus on experience. At the same time, we are seeing a corresponding evolution in the way organizations think about the people they're trying to serve. At the technology stage, organizations spend little or no time thinking about users explicitly—the act of making something possible is enough. When companies focus on features, they tend to view their customers and users in terms of tasks, goals, and preferences. This makes sense; features map pretty clearly onto these concepts. But a focus on experience starts to show the shortcomings of the task/goal/preference model.

Taking a more holistic, experience-focused approach to design means taking a more holistic view of people. What we need are frameworks and terminology that are closer to the ways people talk about and live their lives. To understand people as people, our understanding of our customers and users must better match our understandings of ourselves. After all, our customers aren't so different from us when it comes down to their basic motivations and behaviors. Recognizing this is an important step toward empathy with our customers.

In fact, motivations and behaviors turn out to be a very useful framework for talking about people's lives. If we accept that we need to more directly address emotion, culture, meaning, and context, we find that it's nearly impossible to talk about culture and meaning in terms of tasks and goals. From a more personal perspective, you and I can talk about just about everything we do in our lives in terms of behaviors and motivations. We're motivated to behave in certain ways in the realms of information seeking, banking, or shopping, but also in the realms of love, family, art, and health. We can talk about love and art in terms of tasks and goals, but we diminish the essential spirit of those concepts when we do.

Where we once had tasks, goals, and preferences, we now have discussions of behaviors, motivations, and meaning. This is not just a substitution of one set of words for another; the underlying concepts are different as well. What we're seeing is actually a new way of thinking about people and about design research (Figure 3-4).

Behaviors are the activities in which people engage. Unlike tasks, behaviors need not be focused on a specific goal or outcome. Talking about behaviors rather than tasks allows us to include a much wider range of the activities in people's lives. Motivations lead to, drive, and shape behaviors. We design specifically to support behaviors—just as we've focused on tasks in the past. We use our understanding of underlying motivations to frame the overall user experience. This isn't just about the conceptual model or metaphors of a system, but about understanding the basic drives that lead people to do certain things in certain contexts.

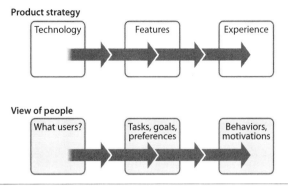

Figure 3-4. Product strategy and understanding of users evolve together. A focus on experience requires a new view of people.

Take an example from some of Adaptive Path's own work. A large bank hired us—call them BankCo—to redesign their online banking system. We approached the project, as good user-centered designers should, with extensive interviewing and field research to understand the financial lives of BankCo's customers. We produced a detailed model of the goals they were trying to accomplish and the tasks they performed to accomplish them. We worked diligently to design features and functions that would make it easy and efficient to meet these goals. We were set up for success, right? Not quite.

You see, around the time we were finishing our analysis, we realized that we were missing something in our model. During the interviews it was fairly obvious that a number of people were misleading us. This wasn't malicious, though. These folks were lying to us *and* to themselves about how well they had a handle on their financial lives.

We saw that when people considered financial products from the bank (loans, lines of credit, new accounts, and so on), they behaved as smart shoppers: comparing options within the bank and across banks; studiously tracking rates and fees. However, they'd inevitably reach a point where they couldn't go any further, and when we probed, we realized that they didn't really understand what they were doing; they were going through the motions of smart shopping, but they had no idea what a successful outcome would be. Probing deeper, we realized that this was predicated on a set of fears when it comes to dealing with financial institutions. Beyond the basic banking tasks that everyone needed to accomplish, people needed to feel empowered and knowledgeable about their finances, but they had no resources or opportunities to get that knowledge and control. If our design didn't come to grips with what *motivated* people's behaviors, it wouldn't ultimately succeed. We were able to use that extra insight to empower and educate people while they were in the midst of normal banking tasks. This project led us to realize that there was something going on behind the tasks and goals.

Embracing Complexity

Albert Einstein once said that "the supreme goal of all theory is to make the irreducible basic elements as simple and as few as possible without having to surrender the adequate representation of a single datum of experience." This is often paraphrased as "theories should be as simple as possible, but no simpler."

With that in mind, it's clear that it is time to improve our models. We know that people aren't simple, yet our theories and models for what makes people tick have been missing a lot of essential data.

If earlier reductionist models offered ways of avoiding or reducing the complexity in people's lives, these new approaches are our attempts to acknowledge and embrace that complexity. By doing so, we are able to understand people more honestly and completely. We gain the potential for greater insights because we see and account for things left out of the old models. We build empathy that gives us the ability to provide a truly great product or service experience. This greater understanding also allows organizations to handle uncertainty and reduce risk. In Chapter 4, we'll explore some of the best ways to go about gaining that understanding. We'll see that understanding customers is not the responsibility of only the research and design team, but of the organization as a whole.

Capturing Complexity, Building Empathy

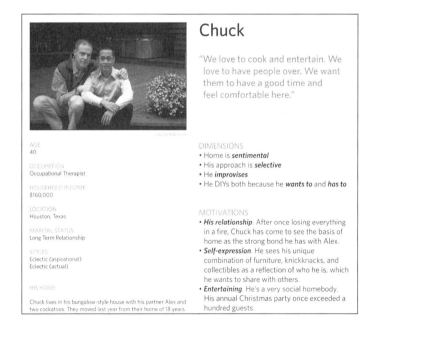

Chuck

"We love to cook and entertain. We love to have people over. We want them to have a good time and feel comfortable here."

AGE
40

OCCUPATION
Occupational Therapist

HOUSEHOLD INCOME
$160,000

LOCATION
Houston, Texas

MARITAL STATUS
Long Term Relationship

STYLES
Eclectic (aspirational)
Eclectic (actual)

HIS HOME

Chuck lives in his bungalow-style house with his partner Alex and two cockatoos. They moved last year from their home of 18 years

DIMENSIONS
• Home is *sentimental*
• His approach is *selective*
• He *improvises*
• He DIYs both because he *wants to* and *has to*

MOTIVATIONS
• *His relationship*. After once losing everything in a fire, Chuck has come to see the basis of home as the strong bond he has with Alex.
• *Self-expression*. He sees his unique combination of furniture, knickknacks, and collectibles as a reflection of who he is, which he wants to share with others.
• *Entertaining*. He's a very social homebody. His annual Christmas party once exceeded a hundred guests.

The success of experience-focused products is contingent on everyone sharing an understanding of users and a vision for the experience, because so many people play a role in delivering that experience.

Creating engaging user experiences requires a solid understanding of the people you want to serve, which inevitably means doing research. Research is a reliable way to gain insight and deal with uncertainty, but to incorporate the ideas from Chapter 3 you may need to reconsider how you think about research. In our experience, a lot of research does nothing but keep research staff busy; however, well-executed research can transform your organization's understanding of its customers, and help your team create compelling experiences.

In this chapter, we'll share what we've learned about how successful, experience-focused companies approach their research efforts. We've already spent a lot of time discussing empathy and the importance of understanding the complexity of your customers' lives. Now, we'll look at some of the methods we use to capture that complexity. We'll also talk about some of the mistakes organizations make with research, and indicators that your research methods could use fine-tuning. Finally, we'll share principles and strategies for successful research.

Of course, every organization has its own needs and idiosyncrasies, so it's impossible to offer step-by-step instructions, but Adaptive Path's strategies have proved effective for our clients and us, even in an increasingly ambiguous market.

Why Research Is Essential

Research for product and service design is about two things: generating ideas and evaluating ideas. It's about answering fundamental questions such as: *What should we make? How should it work? Why should people care?* This is even true once you have tangible designs, prototypes, or completed products and services. Research will augment your work by giving you insight into customers' lives, and helping you develop empathy for them.

Businesses today may use several different types of research:

Evaluative research is a fairly well-understood endeavor, with established disciplines such as human factors, ergonomics, usability, and the like. These fields have developed out of—and have incorporated—a great deal of social and medical science. Their efficacy has been proven over and over because organizations have been doing acceptance tests, usability tests, and market tests for a long time.

Generative research deserves attention because it's a fairly fuzzy endeavor with few clear disciplinary origins. Perhaps this is best indicated by the fact that no one can even agree about what to call it. Your organization probably does some form of "market research" or "user research" as part of its design and development process. But what do these terms mean?

Market research has a fairly established set of techniques (surveys, focus groups, market segmentation), but tends to focus more on what to say than on how a product should work. This can lead to problems, which we'll discuss in more detail later in this chapter.

User research, a term that came out of the world of software and internet applications, is even less clear. It can include anything from observation and interviewing to simply applying evaluative usability techniques at an earlier stage in the process—for example, evaluating earlier versions of a product or offerings from competitors. In our experience, user research has a tendency to be more of the latter than the former.

More recently, design schools and some organizations are championing the term "design research" instead of "user research" or "market research." This term is extremely promising for those of us who are concerned with establishing effective research approaches for design and development. It pushes us out of the purely digital world, and focuses us on the ultimate outcome and measure for research efforts—creating successful products and services. We've been using the term "design research" at Adaptive Path, and will use it as our preferred term for the rest of the book.

Regardless of what you call it, generating ideas for new products and services is fundamentally important to the success of organizations. But keep in mind that research for product and service design isn't about proving theorems or hypotheses. In fact, it's seldom about proving anything. Instead, design research helps establish the constraints and opportunities that make great design possible. Together, the insight and empathy resulting from research provide both a wellspring for ideas and criteria for evaluating those ideas.

Of course, you eventually need to evaluate and develop ideas so they can become real offerings. The methods and strategies we discuss throughout this chapter are applicable for both evaluative and generative research.

Capturing Complexity with Qualitative Research

Chapter 3 made a strong case for the importance of addressing emotion, culture, meaning, and context when we try to understand our customers. When our models of human behavior and motivation are simple, we can get by using primarily quantitative methods like surveys and statistics for research. But once we acknowledge and embrace the complexity of our customers' lives, we need a way to make sense of those intricacies and a means of interpreting the numbers. This isn't a book about research methods, but rather the methodological approaches that organizations use that are critical to the way they understand their customers. So, it's worth taking a moment to review some of the high-level points related to different styles of research.

Quantitative research is useful for understanding trends and getting a sense of *what* is going on. Some quantitative methods can also give you insight into *how* things are happening, but they usually don't tell you *why*. That's because in order to interpret numbers, you need a sense of the mechanisms at play. Otherwise there's no way to know whether a change in a certain number is good, bad, interesting, or trivial.

You can obtain the necessary information through qualitative and contextual research methods, which are specifically geared toward uncovering mechanisms and revealing *why* something is happening. The range of these qualitative and contextual methods is vast, but there are some commonalities among the techniques that can help give a sense of what they are all about. As it turns out, many of these methods are also well-suited to building empathy.

Qualitative research, put most simply, is concerned with the *qualities* of an experience, situation, set of behaviors, and so on, rather than the quantitatively measurable aspects. It focuses on process rather than outcomes—the how and why as opposed to the what, where, and when. Because of the focus on how and why questions, qualitative researchers have to spend a lot of time talking to people. Nearly all forms of qualitative research involve some kind of interviewing. These interviews aren't heavily scripted in an attempt to prove hypotheses by exactly replicating questions and activities across subjects. Rather, they are designed to elicit stories about experiences by responding to what participants say and allowing the conversation to go in unexpected directions. It is more like facilitated storytelling than surveying.

Many qualitative methods are also contextual, meaning that the differences between the spaces and situations in which people live, work, and play are of primary importance. This kind of research is highly inductive—researchers build concepts, hypotheses, and models from the details they uncover in the midst of the research activity. Because it is so inductive, qualitative research is much better at uncovering the unexpected than quantitative approaches. These unexpected discoveries can become a wellspring for original ideas.

For the BankCo project we mentioned in Chapter 3, we began the research expecting to understand the functional and intellectual challenges people have when choosing financial products and services. What surprised us was the role that emotion played in these decisions. People weren't choosing a bank or a specific financial product based on the best fees and rates, but on softer qualities of trust and comfort. This realization led to a set of design recommendations that addressed a potential customer's emotional requirements. These included a streamlined transition between different contact channels (such as email, telephone, branch) so that customers could easily engage in the ways in which they were most comfortable as well as marketing copy that share real-life customer stories.

A subtle and seldom-discussed advantage of qualitative and contextual methods is how they support organizations in developing empathy. Going into people's homes and businesses to talk with them about their behaviors can't help but lead to some connection and understanding of the situation they're in. Making these customers real to the researchers and organization is the first step in developing that connection.

Recently, we've seen a general rise in the popularity and discussion of qualitative methods in design organizations. Terms like interview, observation, field research, contextual inquiry, and ethnography are becoming much more common. It's become standard practice at Adaptive Path to do some qualitative research on nearly every project. Our projects range from internet start-ups to large multi-channel media companies, from non-profits to financial institutions, and from mobile devices to retail spaces. All have benefited from a qualitative approach. This trend is a testament to the importance companies are placing on taking a more holistic, complex, and realistic view of people. It's also evidence for the growing acceptance of culture and context as fundamental to crafting effective customer experiences.

Using Ethnography as a Research Tool

There is no best way to do qualitative research; all of the techniques have their strengths. Most often, the nature of the research question or the situation under study makes one approach more appropriate than another. Still, for many people, the new prominence of qualitative research is closely tied to a specific methodology known as ethnography. Looking at this method in detail can shed light on the use of qualitative approaches in general.

Ethnography is a word you may have heard a lot recently. It's certainly been getting some press. *BusinessWeek*, in particular, has become a champion of ethnography.* In 2006 alone, the magazine published over 15 articles and online posts about the power of ethnography. But what is it, and why are people so excited about it?

Ethnography is a qualitative approach to research focused on gaining a deep understanding of people. It generally involves going into the homes or businesses of the people under study and spending time observing and talking to them. Ethnography differs from other qualitative approaches such as interviews and focus groups in a few important ways. First, it has a strong focus on going out into "the field." Second, because of its roots in anthropology, formally trained ethnographers use social science theory and are particularly focused on cultural and contextual issues. Finally, it delves deeply into study subjects' lives. Academic ethnographers often spend years in their field sites uncovering the subtle details of social and cultural relations and rituals. Thus, ethnography can provide a more realistic view of people, especially with regard to the emotional, contextual, and cultural aspects of their lives.

Of course, ethnography isn't right for every organization or project. It's the most extreme version of the qualitative and contextual methods. True ethnography is quite difficult and requires a good bit of training. It's also incredibly resource and time intensive. In the right situation, it can provide enormous insights that may produce a formidable competitive advantage. But ethnography is overkill for many projects. Even if you do need deep insights, simply hiring ethnographers won't solve your problems. Making effective use of ethnography or other qualitative methods also requires a certain amount of organizational readiness.

---

* "The Science of Desire," *Business Week*, June 5, 2006.

Where Organizations Go Wrong

Before we offer our suggestions for doing effective research that captures complexity and develops empathy, let's look at where organizations go wrong. Below are some common symptoms we've come to associate with organizations whose research efforts aren't as effective as they might be. See if you recognize any of these scenarios.

You might be doing research poorly if:

- You keep making the same mistakes with your customers.

- The functionality or usability of your product is excellent, but sales and usage are low.

- Your products are improved but seldom innovated.

- You have a shelf of reports, and no one knows what's in them.

- Your research team is busy and spending money, but your products don't seem to be getting any more successful.

- The marketing and positioning of products is great but ultimately fail to deliver.

Problems like these tend to result from one or two common faults. Some research fails because the methods aren't appropriate for addressing holistic experiences. Just as often, research fails due to organizational issues; perhaps others in the organization don't see its value or its relevance, or simply don't know how to use it.

Research in Isolation

In many organizations, research is conducted by a department or group that is removed from the rest of the design and development process, both physically and organizationally (Figure 4-1).

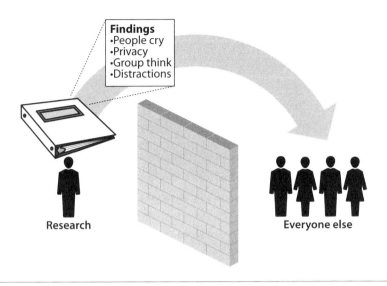

Figure 4-1. How research works in most organizations.

This means that most of the insights are trapped in the research group. If researchers are the only people talking to your customers, the rest of your organization has little opportunity to develop honest empathy. Many research teams receive a set of requirements, go do the research, and then pass the findings back over a figurative (or sometimes actual) wall, in the form of research reports and PowerPoint presentations. Designers, developers, and management read these once, and then file them away on a shelf or in a folder on their computer. This leads us to a second common mistake.

Reports, Where Good Insights Go to Die

Years of experience working on research-intensive design projects have taught the team at Adaptive Path that research reports are generally ineffectual, especially as the sole repository for research. There are lots of reasons why, but it's often simply because the report is so thick you could use it as a doorstop.

*WILKENS' LAW: The effectiveness of a research report is inversely
proportional to the thickness of its binding.*

-Todd Wilkens

This is why organizations accrue shelves of reports that no one ever
uses. Many researchers come from academic or business fields where
research is a matter of proving or defending something; hence, the more
evidence and detail, the better. But the end result of design research
should be fundamentally different from academic research. Design research needs to inspire and indicate a clear direction. It needs to be engaging and powerful. And this isn't just about insights; research should
promote empathy as well. Most reports and presentations aren't effective ways to help others develop empathy.

Market Research versus Design Research

Many organizations make another mistake in the way they approach marketing and design. In theory, market research is simply research focused
on understanding a market or potential market. All organizations do it,
and it makes a lot of sense that they would. But, as we discussed earlier,
the field of marketing has mostly become the field of marketing messages.
It's focused almost exclusively on discovering the stories and ideas that
resonate with people. It sounds sophisticated and postmodern to say that
companies are in the business of selling the idea of things rather than the
things themselves, and it's true that even great products can fail without
good marketing and advertising. At the end of the day, however, most
organizations are making and selling real products and services.

Although we've spent a lot of time talking about intangibles such as
meaning and emotion, your organization creates and provides tangible
offerings. Your customers have a relationship to those products and services that is both tangible and intangible. Just as human factors, ergonomics, and other disciplines have focused too much on the tangible,
marketing tends to focus too much on the intangible. There's clearly
a message and story associated with your offering. But, as Marshall

McLuhan reminded us, the medium (the experience, product, or service) is a fundamental part of the message. It's not just about telling a better or more persuasive story, but also about creating better products and services. Research for the design of products and services is a fundamentally different process than research for messages.

Of course, we don't mean to disparage marketing. On the contrary, we want to help organizations to take advantage of the strengths of traditional marketing research, but also to account for its limitations. Truly effective customer research takes both a traditional marketing approach and a design approach.

Making Research an Organizational Competency

We've found two guiding principles that make research as effective as possible in organizations. Research is successful when:

- It's treated as an *organizational competency*.
- Research outcomes are both *actionable* and *durable*.

When you want to provide a cohesive experience, research must be an organizational competency rather than the job of one person, group, or department. After all, researchers don't actually make products and services; whole organizations do. It's vital to get research insights out of the research department or group and into the organization at large. The success of experience-focused products is contingent on everyone sharing an understanding of users and a vision for the experience, because so many people play a role in delivering that experience. Your business analysts, customer support teams, and retail sales folks should have as much understanding of your customers as your researchers and designers.

Truly effective research work exhibits two traits: it's actionable and durable. Actionable research has clear implications for design, development, marketing, and so on. This ensures that research can influence the work done by these groups. Research that isn't actionable won't have much impact on the products and services being developed. Durable research offers insights that last beyond the research-findings meeting. Otherwise, companies end up having to learn the same things about their customers over and over.

Adaptive Path uses—and recommends—the following strategies to produce actionable, durable results.

Mix Methods

We've spent a lot of time talking about new methods, but we don't mean to say that more traditional and quantitative approaches are unhelpful. What we're saying is that these approaches alone are insufficient. But it is equally true that qualitative methods are insufficient on their own. Taking a mixed method approach is one of the best strategies for ensuring success.

Think of it this way: when you're investing, diversification is an excellent strategy for dealing with the complexities and corresponding uncertainties of the market. The same is true of research. Investing time and resources in a few different approaches will help you identify the important truths of your customers' lives, and help assure you that your organization is on track.

For example, melding market segmentation with interviews and field research can create a more complete picture of your customers. Many organizations have market segmentations based on quantitative analysis of survey data, whether done in-house or purchased from a research firm. These segments generally capture demographics as well as some basic behaviors, especially around purchasing and media consumption. Because they're based on large sample sizes, organizations can feel confident using these patterns as the starting point for planning qualitative research, such as interviews or ethnography. This is an approach we've used successfully at Adaptive Path on many projects. Sometimes we start from quantitative research the organization already has, and sometimes we work with them to craft the surveys. An added benefit of this mixed method approach is that, after developing a richer sense of what's going on with your customers through qualitative research, it's possible to review surveys to explore how widespread observed behaviors and attitudes are. Neither of these approaches alone could provide such comprehensive insight or design inspiration.

Integrate Research with the Design Process

Integrating research into the design and development process is another effective strategy for two reasons. First, your employees need to trust your research before they'll buy in. You can gain trust by bringing people into the process so they understand the origins of your research findings. This is the best way to make research an organizational competency. Second, when it comes to qualitative and contextual research, being there is an integral part of the process. That's why we do research in context in the first place. Just as researchers benefit from being with customers to really appreciate what's going on in their lives, the same is true for the rest of the team. Being in the room brings clarity that is difficult, if not impossible, to communicate via a report or video clip.

Bringing others into the research process is also the surest way to help them develop that honest empathy we keep talking about. Integrating others into research makes empathy a more explicit component and output of the process, every bit as important as the patterns of behavior and motivation you'll uncover. Empathy, in turn, makes your research findings both more durable and more actionable. It's standard practice at Adaptive Path to bring clients, designers, and engineers along with us for field research, or have them call in for phone interviews.

And we aren't the only ones. Big companies like Intel and Samsung have made great strides in this direction as well. Intel has a reputation as a research innovator; it was one of the first large tech companies to hire social scientists to work in research and development through its People and Practices group. Now they've completely restructured the company and put research at the center of their efforts. In these new research-led groups, social scientists and designers work closely on all projects.

Samsung has taken a different approach. In its Global Design Centers, researchers and designers aren't coupled as they are at Intel, but they are located in the same room and work together very closely as a result. Samsung explicitly integrates space, which affords many opportunities for integrated practice.

Unfortunately, these scenarios aren't possible in all organizations; there's a continuum of integration and involvement (Figure 4-2). At one end is the approach we (and Intel) attempt to use on our projects, with people from all parts of the organization involved in the field, in the analysis sessions, and in the sharing and evangelization of the research results. In the middle, you might see organizations where researchers do "share outs," going to other departments to share findings and stories through presentations. At the other end is the bare minimum of involvement. For example, we've had luck on a few projects with just having managers and engineers call in and listen to phone interviews while they worked on something else. Total integration may not happen all at once, but almost any amount of integration will help.

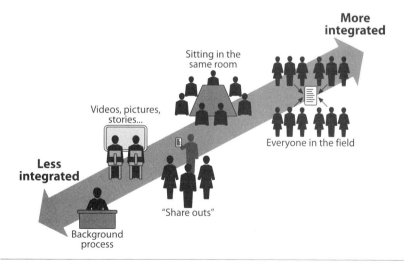

Figure 4-2. There are many different levels of integration between research and design.

Even this little involvement, where the research is essentially a background process for employees, helps your team develop a sense of empathy with the research subjects. Invariably, these managers and engineers will reference something they heard during a phone call to punctuate a behavior, feeling, or story that comes up in research findings. That limited involvement makes research more real to them. In many cases, people who were initially mistrustful of research become enthusiastic advocates in the next round.

Create Truly Useful Deliverables and Artifacts

Unfortunately, sometimes even minimal involvement from key players inside the company is just not a possibility. So, if you can't get everyone involved, you'll have to rely on excellent research artifacts and deliverables. We've found that solid research deliverables exhibit three key characteristics:

- They are clear and straightforward.
- They engage readers.
- They tell stories.

Deliverables should read like histories rather than corporate earnings statements. One particularly effective way to make deliverables more engaging is through the use of *personas,* archetypes of your customers and users that can act as surrogates for those people in the design process (Figure 4-3).

Personas are nothing new, and some people don't think they add much value. But we use them regularly, and have seen them work well for many companies. Well-conceived personas are an efficient way to communicate insights and spark empathy. In our experience, effective personas are drawn from ethnographic research rather than demographics, market segments, or gut feelings about your audience. Your personas should be real, complete, and specific. Name them as individuals rather than as groups, profiles, or stereotypes (i.e., "soccer mom"). Develop personas for specific contexts and projects rather than for use enterprise-wide. To

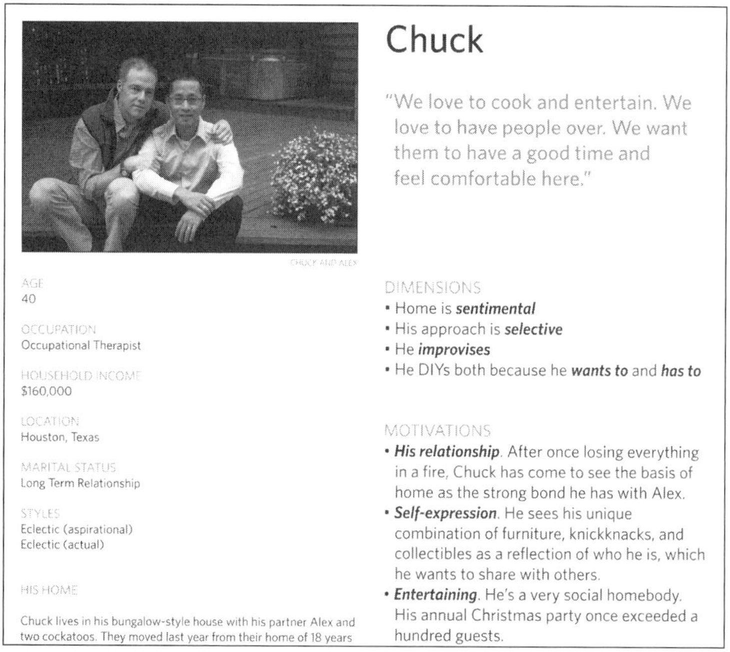

Chuck

"We love to cook and entertain. We love to have people over. We want them to have a good time and feel comfortable here."

CHUCK AND ALEX

AGE
40

OCCUPATION
Occupational Therapist

HOUSEHOLD INCOME
$160,000

LOCATION
Houston, Texas

MARITAL STATUS
Long Term Relationship

STYLES
Eclectic (aspirational)
Eclectic (actual)

HIS HOME
Chuck lives in his bungalow-style house with his partner Alex and two cockatoos. They moved last year from their home of 18 years

DIMENSIONS
• Home is *sentimental*
• His approach is *selective*
• He *improvises*
• He DIYs both because he *wants to* and *has to*

MOTIVATIONS
• *His relationship*. After once losing everything in a fire, Chuck has come to see the basis of home as the strong bond he has with Alex.
• *Self-expression*. He sees his unique combination of furniture, knickknacks, and collectibles as a reflection of who he is, which he wants to share with others.
• *Entertaining*. He's a very social homebody. His annual Christmas party once exceeded a hundred guests.

Figure 4-3. A persona from a project for Scripps Networks HGTV.com.

ensure clarity, keep personas about a page long and include key behaviors and motivations. Personas have names, pictures, and real problems —they're engaging. The best personas also tell their story in their own words, often using quotes from actual research participants.

Quality personas can have far-reaching effects, because organizations can disseminate them to the furthest reaches of their org charts. They also have profound effects on employees beyond the research and design teams. The story about NewsCo from Chapter 3 is a perfect example. In that case, corporate evolution was linked to how strongly personas captured the imagination of that organization. Personas are powerful because they feel real, and they build a human connection.

Research deliverables and artifacts are just part of a larger means of sharing insights and empathy—even personas can't entirely stand alone. Good deliverables are effective only if you make a concerted effort to share them widely. Obviously, these engaging research artifacts work best in organizations that are also making efforts to integrate research.

Make Prototypes

Prototyping isn't usually considered a research activity, but there are few more efficient ways to integrate research into a design and development process. People get engaged when things get tangible, and prototyping helps integrate design, engineering, and marketing into the process, because they're participating in research while it's in progress. You can use prototypes at any stage, and they can take many forms: storyboards, conceptual sketches, or functioning systems, to name a few. Whatever form they take, they give everyone a real-world representation of ideas that will help engender a response from your team.

We worked on a project exploring the relationships people have with their possessions. To tackle such a complex and personal topic, we conducted ethnographic field research and telephone interviews. After the first few sessions with our research participants, we began to have some clear ideas of how the service we were designing might look. Rather than wait until after the "design" phase to explore these ideas, we quickly prototyped the basics of the service using a comic-like storyboard (see Chapter 6 for an example). We shared this story with our research participants during the last 15 minutes of our home visits, just to get a sense of whether the service made sense to them. Based on their reactions, we made slight adjustments to the comic as we went along. This allowed us to mix generative and evaluative research. By the end of the research phase, we had a strong start on the eventual design, and had much stronger buy-in from our clients because the prototype gave us something to share as we worked.

Prototyping products and experiences can also help build empathy with potential users. We worked on a project to develop a new approach to diabetes management. Early on, our team tried to understand the experience of using diabetes management tools by working with a prototype. Several members of the design team spent a few days walking around with a fake insulin pump attached to their stomachs, similar to the one diabetics use daily (Figure 4-4). While there was no way to truly understand what it was like to have diabetes, we came to understand some of the day-to-day difficulties with the related medical equipment. It also helped us to rapidly iterate on designs, seeking solutions that minimized the impact of the traditional tools.

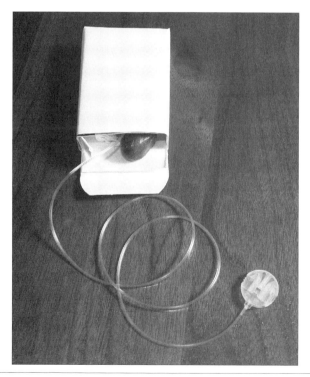

Figure 4-4. A simple prototype of an insulin pump made from a cardboard box and plastic tube, filled with batteries and rocks to approximate weight.

Again, there are no clear step-by-step recipes for research that will work for every organization. The culture of your company and its employees will determine what actually works, but our strategies will give you a foundation and a place to start. Taken together, these research principles and strategies should change the way you regard the researchers in your organization. Their job is not only to learn about customers, but also to ensure that the entire organization shares that knowledge. Companies often think of their researchers as professional learners, but truly effective researchers are teachers and facilitators as well.

CHAPTER 5

Stop Designing "Products"

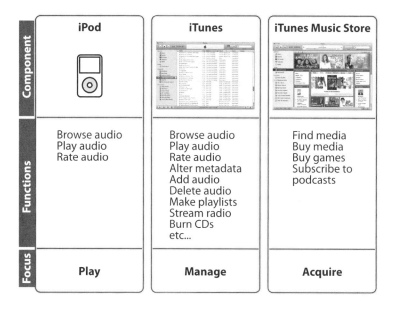

	iPod	iTunes	iTunes Music Store
Component			
Functions	Browse audio Play audio Rate audio	Browse audio Play audio Rate audio Alter metadata Add audio Delete audio Make playlists Stream radio Burn CDs etc...	Find media Buy media Buy games Subscribe to podcasts
Focus	**Play**	**Manage**	**Acquire**

What do people want to accomplish? How does this activity fit into their lives? How can I deliver on those desires? Asking these questions inevitably shifts your focus away from one-off, standalone products and allows you to start thinking of products simply as elements of a much larger system.

Magazines like *BusinessWeek*, *Fast Company*, and *Forbes* have all offered lengthy features on how companies such as Intel, Microsoft, and IDEO watch people in order to understand how to better deliver on unmet needs. What magazine articles rarely discuss is how to take advantage of these observations, or how they can actually guide the development of your offerings.

Remember the story that started this book, about George Eastman and the experience he wanted to deliver with the Kodak camera? If you look at his famous slogan, "You press the button, we do the rest," you'll see that Eastman marketed the camera based on the promise of a drastically simplified experience. But to achieve that result, Eastman needed to do more than merely design a simpler product—that would address only the "you press the button" half of the phrase.

The photographic process is necessarily complicated; it involves loading the camera, exposing light-sensitive material, removing that material, processing the material, and printing images from that material. In this context, just offering a simplified camera wouldn't do enough to alleviate the many challenges of this process. Eastman's genius was in designing his system so customers could focus on what mattered most to them—capturing the image. Photographers no longer had to develop film themselves or pay exorbitant fees to experts. Eastman moved these parts of the photographic process to his developing and processing plant in Rochester, New York (the "we do the rest" part of the equation), thereby allowing the Kodak camera to be remarkably straightforward to use.

An advertisement written in 1888 (Figure 5-1) explains this approach, "A Division Of Labor: After the 100 pictures have been taken, the strip of film (which is wound on a spool) may be removed, and sent by mail to the factory to have the pictures finished."

Figure 5-1. The "Division of Labor" explains that the film can be sent off to be processed, freeing the photographer from such work.

To meet his goal of delivering the ideal customer experience, Eastman realized he needed to develop ongoing relationships with his customers and not just sell a single item. This meant he couldn't think of the Kodak camera as a product, but as a component in a service. This necessitated a factory unlike any seen before, one that could handle complex processing and printing capabilities. Investing in such an operation was an immense risk, but necessary if Eastman wanted to deliver on his promise to "do the rest."

Eastman changed the game by putting his product into a larger system, one where customers sent in their film not only to get their photos processed and printed, but also to get new film loaded onto their old rolls. And unlike other cameras, which were standalone products, his Kodak became a point of entry into a service.

If you're in the market of developing products, the lesson to learn from Eastman is that you need to ask yourself, *What do people want to accomplish? How does this activity fit into their lives? How can I deliver on those desires?* Asking these questions inevitably shifts your focus away from one-off, standalone products and allows you to start thinking of products simply as elements of a much larger system.

Doing It Right

> As a discussion of product design grows longer, the probability of using the iPod as an exemplar approaches one.
>
> > –(With apologies to Mike Godwin).

Over 100 years ago, Eastman's experience-driven, systems approach transformed the field of photography, creating a pre-Kodak and post-Kodak division. Less than a decade ago, digital audio players experienced a similar division, thanks to Apple and its iPod. Though not as fundamental as the shift brought on by Kodak (the iPod had wildly successful portable-audio predecessors, such as the Sony Walkman), the product landscape was permanently altered by the introduction of the iPod in October 2001.

Before then, your portable digital audio choices were CD players, which necessitated carrying stacks of CDs; CD-MP3 players, which required users to rip and burn CDs; flash-drive MP3 players, which at the time had an extremely limited capacity of about 64 MB; or hard-drive MP3 jukeboxes (Figure 5-2). The MP3 options were too expensive or difficult to use for true mass-market adoption, so many people still used CD or audiotape players.

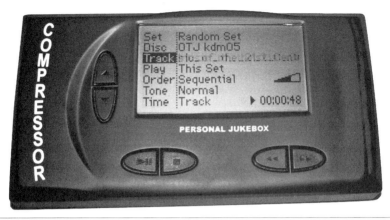

Figure 5-2. The PJB-100 MP3 player offered 5 GB of storage in 1999. Two years later, Apple introduced the iPod, with the same amount of storage.

Much has been written about why the iPod proved successful where others had failed. Typically, it boils down to a superficial discussion of "design," focusing either on the iPod's form—at launch it was smaller than any comparable multi-gigabyte jukebox, and it has an undeniable aesthetic appeal—or its elegant interface and its ability to provide access to thousands of songs.

But the iPod is actually a remarkably limited device. Its basic functions are: browse media, play media, rate media, and change volume level. Heck, it doesn't even have a power button. And I'm paying $250 for that?

The iPod's limitations are even more remarkable when you consider that the standard practice in consumer electronics is to cram as many functions as possible into a single device—have you used a mobile phone lately? Marketers insist that people want more and more features, and product designers assume that each device must stand alone in the world, capable of doing everything on its own. Apple, however, borrowed a page from Eastman's playbook and bucked the trend.

In the same way that Eastman simplified the customer's experience down to "You press the button, we do the rest," Apple clearly had an experience strategy for the iPod from the outset: all your music, any time, anywhere. (Over time, "music" has evolved to the more all-inclusive "media.") Everything about the continuing design and development of the iPod supports this one goal. In fulfilling this goal, Apple's genius wasn't in the design of form or interface, but in the design of the entire system that supports the media consumer.

This system can be broken down into three segments: acquire media, manage media, and listen to or watch media (Figure 5-3). The iPod device focuses on delivering the minimal set of functionality desired by someone on the go—playing media. Since Apple could assume that everyone with an iPod has a computer (it's the only way to get media onto the iPod), Apple could place all other necessary functions in a piece of software—iTunes.

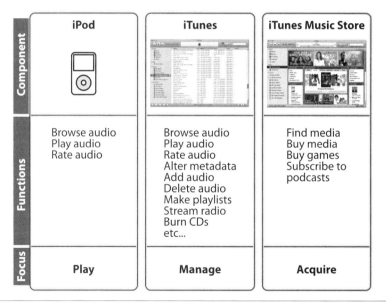

Figure 5-3. Placing functionality across the system where appropriate is the secret to the iPod's success.

iTunes allowed the iPod to be a simple and elegant device. This key strategy of allowing software to manage the bulk of functionality is often underappreciated. The iPod doesn't need to let you delete media, or rename items, or create playlists. Those "manage media" functions are handled far more efficiently by iTunes, with its big display, and a keyboard and mouse as input devices. Thus, iPod can provide very little functionality and still be a massive success.

That leaves us with the last segment of the system—acquire media. For the first year and a half of the iPod's existence, users acquired media either through purchasing CDs and ripping them, or by illegally downloading files. But that whole time, Apple was talking to music labels, and finally, in April 2003, Apple launched the iTunes Music Store (now called iTunes Store), supplying the third and final piece of the puzzle. Built into the iTunes application, the store lets you acquire media almost as easily as iTunes lets you manage it, or an iPod lets you play it. These three distinct components allow functionality to concentrate where it's most appropriate; and perhaps more importantly, shift unnecessary functionality so it doesn't get in the way where it isn't needed.

Though distinct, these segments seamlessly connect. This is perhaps best expressed by how an iPod automatically syncs to iTunes when connected to a computer—no need to even push a button, a requirement of earlier syncing devices such as the Palm. Because these components complement one another so well, the success of each reinforces the others. iTunes is better for having a device like the iPod to play music on; the iPod is better for having software like iTunes to do the heavy lifting. As a direct result of the design of this entire media system, Apple has withstood intense competitive pressure, and still dominates not only the digital media player market (even if you measure conservatively, Apple has over 60 percent), but also the legally-obtained media download market (Apple's share is over 80 percent, and in June 2007, it became the third-largest music retailer in the United States, behind Wal-Mart and Best Buy*).

Like Eastman Kodak, Apple has prevailed by delivering on an experience strategy. Apple's approach to delivery differs from Kodak in that they don't hide complexity from their customers. Instead they leverage components across a system, so that the experience never becomes too complex. With digital systems, you can appropriately give people a lot of power and control. The trick is to approach the offering as a system whose components have narrowly defined functions, so that the experience is never overwhelming.

Maintaining Focus

Given Apple's intense competitive pressure, expanding the functionality of iTunes and iPod would be an understandable response. Since its launch, competitors have offered numerous features not found on the iPod, including voice recording, FM radio tuning, and Wi-Fi connectivity.

Yet Apple has responded by adding almost no functionality. Apart from the store, iTunes's biggest innovation was Party Shuffle, which plays your music in random order. What it has added is support for new types of media—podcasts, television, movies, audiobooks, games—but the core functionalities are still mostly browse and play. The iPod's only significant change has been the option for greater and greater storage.

Such functional stasis fits within that experiential strategy mentioned before: all your media, any time, anywhere. An FM tuner wouldn't provide *your* media. In fact, the whole point of the iPod calls into question the necessity of FM radio. Who needs crappy music stations when you can program your own? And what about voice recording? Well, apart from itinerant reporters, how many people would actually use it?

---

* "Apple Rises to No. 3 Music Seller in U.S.," *Los Angeles Times*, June 22, 2007.

With the release of iPod Touch, Apple is now offering Wi-Fi connectivity. But unlike Microsoft's Zune, which used Wi-Fi to make music social (to little success), Apple positioned Wi-Fi on iPod Touch as a means of downloading songs from iTunes, video from YouTube, and accessing your favorite web sites. As such, it's all still about your media.

This is where experience strategy and systems design intersect. In designing a system, you can get caught up in all the opportunities that technology makes available. A strong experience strategy makes clear not just what to do, but what *not* to do.

Doing It Wrong: A Classic Mistake

A couple of years ago, Adaptive Path was approached to consult on the design of a new service to be offered in a line of digital music keyboards. Our client, which I will call KeyboardCo, had a smart idea to enhance the extensibility of their keyboards by enabling the download of songs and music lessons through the Internet. On the face of it, this idea—turn the product into a service that evolves with person playing the keyboard—sounded brilliant.

Unfortunately, their design and development process didn't start with defining the experience they wanted to deliver. Instead, KeyboardCo committed the classic product designer mistake: they approached the addition of new functionality (Internet connectivity) as simply a feature to check off a list of requirements. In the process, they crammed all of the functionality into the keyboard, believing that the product had to be able to stand alone. They even touted it in their marketing, "Connect to the Internet from your keyboard—without a PC!" The user plugged an Internet adapter into the keyboard's USB port to connect to the network.

Sadly, by the time KeyboardCo came to us they were committed to this approach. Because the music keyboard's hardware was not designed to browse the Internet, they now needed help figuring out how to retrofit the existing display and buttons for Internet connectivity. The challenges to overcome included:

- Small, 320 x 240 pixel screen

- No typewriter keyboard to enter characters

- No mouse or trackball for freely moving the cursor

- No touch screen

For input, all we had to work with was a row of vertical ATM-like buttons on either side of the screen, and a jog dial. Given this constraint, the interface we came up with looked like an ATM screen—hardly an optimal way to browse the Internet, but the best we could devise under the circumstances. When users needed to type something (say, their login information), they rotated the jog dial, which moved a cursor over a graphical display of a typewriter keyboard. When the cursor was over the correct letter, users clicked a button to "type" it.

Obviously, the user's experience was ridiculous. One project for the client was to conduct in-home observations of the "out-of-the-box experience"—what was it like to set it up and connect it to the Internet? While people had no trouble plugging it in and turning it on, no one was able to connect it to the Internet without help. Why? Remember how you connect the keyboard to the Internet? With a USB adapter. No one had the USB adapters at home, and very few realized that such a thing even existed. If we hadn't been there to hand them USB adapters so that we could continue our observations, no one would have been able to connect.

Our observations revealed an interesting circumstance. The few people who understood the USB port connection all had the same thought: why not connect the music keyboard to their computer? What these people intuited was what the product designers missed—they already had a device connected to the network, a device very well-suited to browsing the Internet. And KeyboardCo didn't realize that anyone paying over $1,000 for a digital music keyboard was almost sure to have a computer as well.

Had the product's designers stepped back and considered the whole system of supporting people who play music on their keyboards, it's likely that they would have come up with a solution similar to Apple's: use the PC for browsing and purchasing music, and use the device to play it. This all seems so obvious that it feels bizarre to point it out. But considering that this very successful company spent millions of dollars on this technology and the service to back it up, it's easy to imagine that other companies are making mistakes just as—if not more—grave.

Doing It Right Online

Kodak, Apple, and even KeyboardCo are all examples of products-as-services with physical components—cameras, music players, keyboards. Also, they're able to control most, if not all, of the system: Kodak makes the cameras, the film, and the paper; Apple sells iPod, develops iTunes, and opens the iTunes Store; KeyboardCo makes the pianos and retails the downloadable music.

Such situations are rare. Many companies simply can't control the system in which they find themselves. Instead, we're seeing a marketplace increasingly filled with functional components that demand greater interconnectedness. Web products, particularly those found under the rubric of "Web 2.0," offer the best examples of how to enter a market by integrating with a larger system outside of your control.

This is best demonstrated in the burgeoning online photo-sharing space. 1999 saw the launch of the Web's significant photo sites: Ofoto, Shutterfly, and Yahoo! Photos. These were all responses to the increasing popularity of digital cameras, and the challenge of sharing those photos and making quality prints.

Skip ahead to 2004, when the digital photography market became surprisingly complex. Sales of digital cameras surpassed film cameras. People's hard drives were full of images. Camera phones became increasingly popular, but it was unclear what to do, exactly, with the pictures you snapped with your phone. Customers were going in all directions in terms of what they wanted to do with their photos. Some wanted to share them with the world, others only with friends and family; some wanted prints, others were happy with displaying their photos on-screen. An increasing number of bloggers wanted to use imagery to enhance their stories, or simply to augment their online personas. And people had hundreds, or even thousands, of photos in need of organizing.

Unfortunately, the photo sites of 2004 hadn't really evolved with the times. They continued focusing on uploading digital camera pictures and turning them into prints or gifts. They offered no services geared at folks with camera phones, and little support for people who simply wanted to share photos digitally. Organization was restricted to two anachronistic models—rolls and albums.

Into this maelstrom plunged Flickr, which launched in the first few months of 2004. From the start, Flickr was never a standalone application; its creators knew they had to rely on the larger digital photographic system to succeed. In fact, Flickr emerged as an interface to this system, coordinating components that had been built separately, tying them together in a giant open database. These components included digital cameras; photo management software like Picasa and iPhoto; cameraphones and their ability to email photos; personal publishing tools such as Blogger, Typepad, and WordPress; and photo printing services.

Flickr sits at the hub of potential chaos. Yet anyone who has used the system knows that it has remarkable coherence. How does it not fracture in the face of such functionality?

Flickr is driven by two explicit experience strategies, clearly presented on its About Page (Figure 5-4) (*http://www.flickr.com/about/*):

1. We want to help people make their photos available to the people who matter to them.

2. We want to enable new ways of organizing photos.

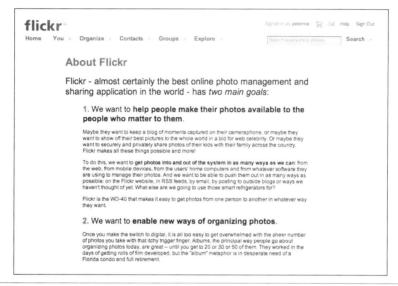

Figure 5-4. Flickr's "About" page makes explicit the two fundamental elements of Flickr's experience strategy.

The About page continues with this very telling sentence, "To do this, we want to get photos into and out of the system in as many ways as we can: from the Web, from mobile devices, from the users' home computers and from whatever software they are using to manage their photos." Flickr understands that you have a collection of tools you're already happy using, and it has no desire to replicate the functionality of those tools; it wants to capitalize on their functionality to offer new opportunities for sharing.

Actually, Flickr does want to replicate, or rather surpass, the functionality of one kind of existing tool—photo management software. The folks behind Flickr recognize that existing management tools are stuck in outmoded ways of considering pictures as rolls and albums. Digital camera users commonly have hundreds or thousands (or hundreds of thousands!) of photos, and these vast collections need to be managed with more robust means. And so Flickr stepped up with tagging, photo sets, groups, and maps, providing unique ways of organizing pictures. Adaptive Path is an all-Mac shop, but when people here want to look at their personal photo collections, they don't launch iPhoto; it's too unwieldy. They log in to Flickr.

A Strategic Choice

Eastman Kodak and Apple had to create whole systems of support because there was simply nothing out there to leverage. However, it's worth noting that for all the closed aspects of their system, Apple made the crucial choice to support the open technology of MP3. Other portable players supported MP3, but at the time of iPod's launch, it was conceivable that a company like Apple would have been tempted to use a proprietary format. They wouldn't have been alone: when Sony launched its "iPod Killer," the NW-HD1, it required files in Sony's proprietary format, something called ATRAC3. Apple realized that the iPod had to work easily with the tons of audio already on people's hard drives—remember the experience strategy: *your media*, any time, anywhere"—and thus committed to MP3.

By understanding what people actually want to do with their photos, the folks behind Flickr developed a two-pronged experience strategy to define their service. Inherent in that strategy is an appreciation that Flickr cannot stand alone as competing online photo sites or photo management software applications have attempted. Flickr must work as a component of the existing digital photography ecosystem. As a measure of its success, Yahoo!, which acquired Flickr in 2005, announced in May 2007 that they were scrapping Yahoo! Photos and moving all accounts over to Flickr.

When Services Behave Like Products

If a secret of success for products in today's market is to behave more like a service, then companies that are already in the service industry should have an advantage as they develop tools to help their customers. Sadly, as any customer of a bank, hospital, insurance company, cable company, or utility knows, this is rarely the case. Why is it that these organizations, supposedly designed around their relationships with their customers, fail so badly when providing tools to help those customers?

At Adaptive Path, we had a financial services firm (let's call them FinanceCo) ask us to redesign their customer web site, the place where customers log in, check their accounts, move money around, and maybe trade stocks or open an IRA. Only about 20 percent of their customers used the web site, even though they knew that most of their customers had computers with Internet access.

To understand the context for which we were designing, we conducted 15 in-home interviews with current FinanceCo customers. Nearly all of them griped about their monthly statements. The statements were unwieldy, overlong, and dense with information that didn't make sense to them. The customers simply looked at the first page, felt assured that the number was around where they thought it should be, and ignored the rest.

When customers wanted to do anything, such as move money or trade stocks, they picked up the phone and called their personal advisor. No task was too small when it came to involving advisors. And the advisors, who wanted to maintain a sense of control over the relationship with customers, were happy with this setup.

Our observations revealed that FinanceCo treated every customer touchpoint (industry jargon for the points at which the service "touches" the customer, such as a monthly mailed statement, web site, or a phone call to the financial advisor) as a wholly separate silo. That's why the monthly statement was 20 pages long and filled with information, instead of focusing on the core information of interest to most customers, and encouraging those customers who seek details to use the Web to probe more deeply. We also learned that, inside the organization, the people designing the statement didn't coordinate with those designing the web site. Since these silos didn't interact, each silo had to provide as many services (or, if we were talking about products, functions) as possible. And so functionality was replicated across the touchpoints (Figure 5-5).

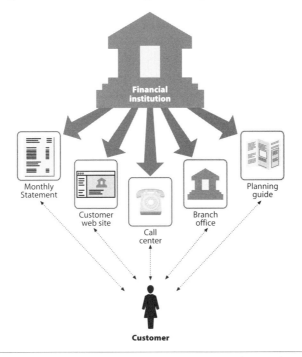

Figure 5-5. A customer's experience extends across multiple touchpoints, but organizational silos can prevent those touchpoints from coordinating effectively.

What this meant for us is that no matter how much we improved the web site through redesign, its impact would be mitigated by the performance of the other touchpoints. As long as the monthly statements were so frustrating that customers threw their hands up in dismay, reinforcing their belief that it wasn't worth engaging directly with FinanceCo, the web site would underperform. As long as customers felt obliged to engage their advisors for menial tasks, the web site would underperform.

We explained to FinanceCo that they needed to treat all these touchpoints as components in a coherent system. And, as we saw with Kodak and Apple, that system had to have two key objectives: 1) allow customers to accomplish their goals, by 2) moving the functionality to where it was most appropriate in the system.

Our primary recommendation was to redesign across the touchpoints, with an eye to the customer's experience. The statement would be simplified to focus only on the essential information that customers sought. The advisors would be called upon only for help executing deeper tasks which actually required the assistance of a human brain—things like portfolio planning and allocation, or large loans. The web site would fill a middle ground between these two. The Web is great for presenting detailed information when it's actually desired, so all that overwhelming content that previously choked the monthly statement could instead be called up online, if and when it was needed. The web site would also take care of the menial tasks that don't require a human—moving money from account to account, opening up a small account, and other day-to-day financial tasks.

This division of labor would allow each touchpoint to play to its strengths, and prevent frustration by removing inappropriate functionality from the touchpoints that don't require it.

Symphony or Cacophony?

In our discussions with our direct clients at FinanceCo, we realized that the primary reason for the lack of service coordination was their organizational structure. When we recommended to our direct clients in the Interactive Marketing Group that they needed to engage in a design effort across the entire customer experience, they nodded and understood, but were powerless to do anything. They didn't really know the folks who developed and designed the monthly statements. They had very little interaction with the team that managed relationships with advisors. All they had was their charter, which was limited to the web site design. And frankly, they had too few people working on that, so there was no way extra effort would be expended to cross silos and satisfy a holistic customer experience.

Now, Adaptive Path isn't an organizational consulting company. We know it's extremely hard to change organizations to accommodate new realities. We also know that it seems awfully glib to say that to succeed, each customer-facing channel in an organization needs to stop being a walled-off silo, and become an instrument in a coordinated symphony that addresses the whole customer experience.

Still, to fully succeed, each customer-facing channel needs to stop being a walled-off silo and become an instrument in a coordinated symphony that addresses the whole customer experience. The problem facing big corporations is that they are structured to optimize efficiency and operations, typically around the repeated delivery of the same product or service. This structure runs exactly counter to what's needed in a truly customer-facing organization, which requires that products or services continually evolve to meet customers' needs (Figure 5-6).

Eastman Kodak and Apple were able to succeed in large part because they had no preexisting organizational structure to overcome. Eastman created an industry out of whole cloth, and therefore was able to build an organization specifically to meet its demands. Apple was getting into new spaces (consumer electronics and media retail), and could approach them fresh. The company that should have dominated the mobile media space, Sony, couldn't, because it required coordination of existing units with distinct modes of operation.

Figure 5-6. Such hierarchical organization charts support delivery of existing services, but actually inhibit addressing newly realized customer needs.

Don't Over-Engineer

It's tempting when designing systems to specify every last detail. Some believe that to ensure the smoothest experience they must control all of the elements. However, it's important to remember that we are not and should not be completely in charge of these experiences. While it's important to coordinate your efforts to craft coherent, coordinated systems, when it comes to designing for experience, there is a surprisingly fine line between delight and dictatorship, between total experience design and totalitarianism. You have to be careful not to over-architect or over-engineer experiences and the systems that drive them.

A cautionary note comes from Adam Greenfield, author of the book *Everyware: The Dawning Age of Ubiquitous Computing*, in an essay in which he describes what has ultimately been the failure of Amtrak's Acela train service, in spite of the fact that the experience was designed from end to end by IDEO.[*]

> *IDEO divided [the train riding experience] into ten distinct phases; their conception of an Acela trip began even before passengers had necessarily settled on traveling by train, accounted for the rituals of arriving at the station and purchasing tickets, and followed until they had transferred to another mode of transportation upon arrival at the destination...*
>
> *The assumptions embedded in the plan are too tightly coupled to one another. They feed from one to the next—remember the word—seamlessly, like brittle airline timetables so tightly scheduled that a delay anywhere in the densely-interwoven mesh of connections cascades through the entire system. When it all succeeds, it's magnificent, but if any aspect of it fails, the whole thing falls apart...*
>
> *...Designers may well be able to specify the degree to which a seat reclines, the font in which a sign is set, or the sleek lines of a uniform— but not the behavior of the person in that uniform, and ultimately, that's far more likely to determine the tenor of any experience. Acela's lesson for experience designers is simple, one that most of us learned in childhood: don't bite off more than you can chew.*

You have to recognize that a system will degrade, and make it such that such entropy doesn't shatter the entire experience. The true success of experience design isn't how well it works when everything is operating as planned, but how well it works when things start going wrong.

One way to ensure such resilience is to let users of the system leave an impression. This is one of the lessons of the Web 2.0 movement that should be applied in contexts other than that of digital technologies.

---

[*] "On the Ground Running: Lessons from Experience Design," Adobe Design Center's Think Tank, May 2007.

Kodak:
Where Is It Now?

For over 100 years, Eastman Kodak dominated the consumer photography industry. Their cameras might have lost favor to top Japanese brands, but their film and processing maintained huge market share into the 1990s. The system that Eastman designed continued to serve the experiential mantra of "You press the button, we do the rest."

Then, as the 1990s progressed, digital photography emerged. And Kodak was nowhere to be found. It became clear that Kodak wasn't really about satisfying the photographer's experience. Kodak had forgotten the lesson George Eastman taught—understand what the customer wants to accomplish, and design a system to accommodate that.

Kodak couldn't imagine doing anything that might harm its primary businesses of film and photo paper. As a result, digital initiatives went underfunded, and Kodak was unprepared for the digital revolution.

Eventually Kodak saw the writing on the wall and dove into digital photography wholeheartedly. Employing squads of researchers and designers, they realized a key experiential challenge that their core audience faced when it came to digital photography—how to get those photos off a camera and onto a computer? Kodak launched the EasyShare line of cameras, which rapidly became the bestselling digital camera brand. The customer experience orientation that had served them so well in the past once again came through.

But...not so fast—digital cameras, it turns out, offer weak profit margins. Even with all of its sales success, Kodak wasn't making enough money to overcome the lost profits from film and paper. Kodak made the classic product company mistake; they innovated on the standalone product. If they were really going to follow in Eastman's august footsteps, they needed to create an innovative system that supported the entire spectrum of digital photographer needs.

Ultimately, instead of providing a seamless environment, you want to provide meaningful, beautiful seams into which people can insert themselves, customizing their experiences to suit their needs.

In his book *How Buildings Learn*, Stewart Brand notes that all buildings are predictions and that all predictions are wrong.[*] The same is true of all designed things. But this need not lead to fatalism. The buildings, products, or services we create can be designed and used so that it doesn't matter when they're wrong. He also makes the case that the most important thing when creating something that can accommodate uncertainty is to have a strategy: "Where a plan is based on prediction, a strategy is designed to encompass unforeseeably changing conditions."[†] Think back to Chapter 2, where we stressed the importance of an experience-based strategy. Such articulations will allow you to successfully respond when new circumstances arise, by orienting everyone toward a common goal.

The System Is the Product

The key message here is not to approach a design problem assuming you'll create a product, a service, and a system. Begin with the experience you want to design for, and then—and only then—identify the components that will deliver it.

By doing that, you will likely realize that the most desirable approach is to create an interface into a larger system, whether that system is one of your own design or a preexisting product that you incorporate into your experience. Eastman designed a system with his Kodak camera that provided simple access to the complexity of photography, with his factories doing the heavy lifting of processing and printing. Apple provided multiple interfaces to its system for enjoying media, but coordinated them so the customer never felt overwhelmed at any particular point. On the

---

[*] Stewart Brand, *How Buildings Learn: What Happens After They're Built* (Penguin, 2001), p 178.

[†] Stewart Brand, ibid., p. 178.

other hand, FinanceCo also provided multiple interfaces to their financial services, but the lack of coordination between all these elements meant that each interface engaged the full complexity of the system, and ultimately left its customers overwhelmed.

These various successes and struggles clearly demonstrate the need to stop thinking of anything you design as a standalone product. You have to address the experience at large, whether that means building out a system of your own design or tapping into a preexisting setup. Most importantly, make sure that each aspect of the overall experience complements the others, doing nothing more or less than the customer needs.

CHAPTER 6

The Design Competency

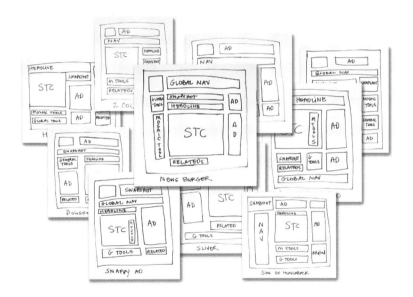

*The act of design gives form to a powerful
idea that many can rally around.*

So there we have it: the secret sauce is to focus on experiences by delving into the complexities of people's lives, and then to create elegant systems to support them. This is where this book could and would end if it were really all that easy to do. Of course, it isn't easy. In fact, it can be painfully hard.

Obstacles to Adopting Experience Design

Take the Diamond Rio. It was one of the first digital music players to hit the market, well before the iPod, and it was way ahead of the curve. Around the time of its introduction, the market for MP3s and digital music was rapidly expanding, despite the Recording Industry Association of America's best attempts to squash the trend with lawsuits. Diamond Multimedia had correctly identified a potential market for devices to store and play this enormous stockpile of digital music. But Diamond was never able to rally wide adoption. The Rio's features made logical sense, but it just never struck a chord with the public.

Diamond had the right business case. They understood the opportunity and had the technology, but they didn't deliver a digital music experience that resonated with customers. Diamond learned a painful lesson: the ability to create a new technology isn't synonymous with the ability to craft a desirable customer experience.

Once an organization decides to focus on experiences, it seems that doing so should be easy. There may be talk of doing it, plans to do it, and meetings to coordinate the doing. Unfortunately, processes, procedures, cross-departmental coordination, reviews, and planning meetings get in the way. Procedural overhead can be a huge obstacle to progress.

However, there are upsides to overhead: it reduces unnecessary risks, ensures a level of reliability and coherence, lowers the number of complete duds that make it to market, and generally prevents organizations from running around like a bunch of headless chickens. Everyone needs some level of organization and rigor to figure out how to approach a problem.

Still, many companies are unable to balance the *managing* with the *doing*, because they're busy engaging in all the trappings of productivity. Holding meetings, running reports, fixing bugs, writing emails, and sharing PowerPoint presentations—these are widely understood commodity skills, and people usually look good when they're doing them because it makes them appear productive. People rarely try to create something new, because untried methods are often difficult for others to understand and thus have the potential to fail.

This is one of the reasons that organizations resist practicing design, especially the practice of designing something as ethereal as experiences. The components of experience design appear incompatible with the common practices of organization management: objectivity, measurement, and control.

Companies often invest heavily in quantitative analyses and objective management controls, but dedicate minimal resources to understanding and improving their design processes. The irony is that a sound design process results in desirable products and services, which in turn make marketing, managing, and measuring so much easier. That reality can get lost in the quest to optimize.

Take the last seven years at 3M, for example. Under new leadership, the organization, which devised Post-It notes and masking tape, dedicated itself to popular optimization practices while its creative muscles atrophied. The company once derived a third of its sales from recently developed products (those created in the last five years), but that figure quickly slipped to a fourth as the pipeline of new ideas began to dry up.

As *BusinessWeek* said of 3M, "While process excellence demands precision, consistency, and repetition, innovation calls for variation, failure, and serendipity." [*]

Even companies well-invested in the design process can encounter huge barriers when they attempt to focus on experience. The key is to zero in on qualitative customer insights, which can be trickier to incorporate than quantitative optimization practices.

One way to acclimate an organization to experience design is to focus on people's real lives. However, as we pointed out in Chapter 3, organizations tend to see the customer as an aggregated number on a top-line marketing report, a voice at a focus group, or a *cha-ching* at the register. Employees and business owners spend time in boardrooms, meeting rooms, studios, and airplanes, not in their customers' living rooms. For experience design to prevail, business owners, marketers, engineers, designers, and sales staff all need to develop a deep appreciation for how customers' real-life experiences should inform everyday organizational decisions.

Understanding and Affecting Experience

Business management is obsessed with attributes that can be measured and improved: return on investment, share of market, productivity. Even the notion of quality has been defined and converted into formulas so that businesses can better manage this subjective attribute.

Experience sometimes fails to gain traction because it's tough to quantify, and you can't point at it. Yet "great user experience" always appears as a bullet in the PowerPoint presentation for every new product and service that gets pitched to upper management. Few organizations move beyond the bullet point because a great experience is difficult to plan for, and almost impossible to spec.

---

[*] Brian Hindo, "At 3M, A Struggle Between Efficiency and Creativity" *Business Week*, June 11, 2007.

Good Experiences Require Systemic Coordination

Organizations may find a system view far more accessible than an experience view. After all, systems need organizing, and infrastructure demands management. But even within a system view, organizations still have considerable difficulty planning and executing systems across channels and organizational silos.

The functional dependencies of systems are well understood, and organizations generate reams of system architecture diagrams. Rarely do they create such maps from a customer perspective, even though it's imperative that companies know what happens to customers who are trying to piece together a couple of touchpoints into solutions for their individual situations.

By definition, systems are composed of multiple components. To deliver value to the customer and the organization, systems must be greater than the sum of their parts. For instance, it's not enough that my mobile phone has wireless communications, an address book, and access to a voicemail system. These must work together to create value, and that takes real effort. It reportedly took Apple and Cingular months to create the iPhone's voicemail system which presents messages organized by the names of the callers from your address book. With a system like this, a great experience takes a considerable effort to integrate the components, as well as a clear vision of how integration will add value.

As we've already mentioned, sometimes the additive process of creating or expanding a system can run amok. If a few components are good, then adding a few more will be excellent. But with each additional component, complexity grows exponentially. The more you add to a system, the more ways it can fall apart and confuse customers. It takes strength and perseverance to prevent systems from succumbing to feature creep.

Good experience requires not just an understanding and coordination of a system, but a coordination of that system from the perspective of the customer's experience. Let's call the organization that follows this experience-driven approach the Type-X Organization.

Type-X Organizations are extremely hard to create and sustain. First, the customer perspective must be understood widely and considered often. Unfortunately many employees in large organizations go years without seeing a customer. Second, products and services must be managed and presented as a series of related experiences, not as features occupying a market gap. But assessing needs and delivering solutions from this more qualitative perspective challenges most conventional business wisdom. Third, measuring and proving the value of experience-driven changes is difficult, although not impossible. Sadly, however, most organizations prefer to gauge their progress using the same metrics as their competitors.

The Trouble with New, Better, and Different

Perhaps the biggest barrier to developing great experiences is a very simple issue: it's difficult to do things that are new, better, and different. First of all, it's hard to find something that your competitors don't already offer. It can feel like the competition has organically expanded into every possible market niche.

Yet markets are often quickly thrust into change by new offerings and experiences. Discount airlines and online booking have changed the airline industry, if not the entire travel industry. Craigslist has upended the world of classified ads, delivering a devastating blow to the newspaper industry. Apple is now the third largest music retailer in the United States. The rise of the Barnes and Noble superstores, concomitant with the establishment of Amazon.com, rang a death knell for independent booksellers. All these offerings earned success in over-saturated markets because they found new solutions to old problems.

Second, your offering has to be compelling to customers. Creating something new is easy when compared with creating something *desirable*. Too often "innovation" is associated with novel or even cavalier concepts, created to fulfill a customer need that doesn't exist and never will. Marketers then have to try to convince customers that they have needs that don't exist, rather than simply connecting people with products and services that obviously address their needs.

Third, your offering can't be easily imitated or you quickly lose your advantage. New offerings based on cosmetic or commodity features will quickly land you in a parity war, leaving you scrambling to match competitors feature for feature. It takes considerable industry knowledge and investment to discover and build capabilities that are unique and hard to replicate. But the results can give you a long-term advantage: it took Blockbuster years to come close to matching Netflix's ability to deliver DVDs through the mail (Figure 6-1).

Figure 6-1. Netflix created a new and more convenient way for people to rent DVDs.

It's a feat to create something new, compelling, and hard to imitate, and then find a way to bring it together and take it to market. Yet these elements are at the core of successful competitive strategy and innovation.

What's Missing?

If delivering a differentiated, coordinated system that responds to real customer needs is the core of great user experiences, then why don't organizations have processes in place that allow them to do this?

Most companies are absolutely capable of creating the necessary processes. It's just that this capability has languished because design activities have been discouraged in standard business practice. The ability to design and create new experiences is diffused and scattered throughout every technical and creative discipline. In addition, it's typically relegated to the lowest levels of an organization, given the least thought and analysis, and, not surprisingly, produces results that are well beneath its potential.

It's also easy for organizations to convince themselves that they deliver good experiences to their customers, when that may not be the case. In 2005, business consultancy Bain & Company surveyed U.S. businesses, asking them if they thought they delivered superior customer experiences. Eighty percent of the surveyed companies said they did, so the researchers asked the customers of those companies the same question. On the whole, the customers didn't agree; they felt that only 8 percent of those companies delivered superior customer experiences (Figure 6-2).[*]

---

[*] James Allen, Frederick F. Reichheld, Barney Hamilton, and Rob Markey, "Closing the Delivery Gap: How to Achieve True Customer-Led Growth" *Results Brief Newsletter*, Bain & Company, October 5, 2005.

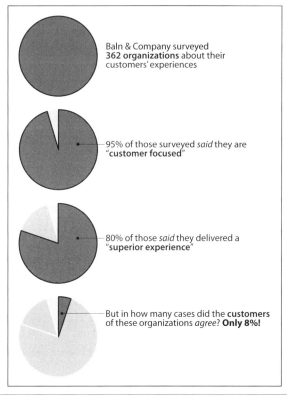

Baln & Company surveyed **362 organizations** about their customers' experiences

95% of those surveyed *said* they are **"customer focused"**

80% of those *said* they delivered a **"superior experience"**

But in how many cases did the **customers** of these organizations *agree*? **Only 8%!**

Figure 6-2. Organizations' belief that they deliver great experiences is far from the truth.

About Design

We are all designers. Whether at home—in your kitchen, in your garden, in your closet—or at work, we all arrange separate elements to suit a particular purpose. Because design is so commonly practiced, everyone in your organization can participate when necessary. True, you may have come across a few inflexible, prima-donna designers in your time, unwilling to compromise on a particular curve or color. But although some designers seem inflexible, the actual act of designing is nimble and can be blended with other rigorous organizational processes.

- **Design is humanistic.** It assumes a viewer, an operator, a user, a customer, and a context. The decisions made in the practice of design are based on what works best when someone uses a design. The more insight you have into the use and the user, the better a design becomes. Malcolm Gladwell's book, *The Tipping Point*, illustrates this with the story of Nickelodeon's show for preschoolers, *Blue's Clues*. The producers of this popular and effective educational show disassembled the long-time educational leader *Sesame Street*, determined which aspects worked best for kids, spent time with children to understand why these elements of the show were so successful, and then focused on making those learning experiences even more effective than before. Each script and show of *Blue's Clues* is tested with children three or four times before it's ever aired. It's this natural, responsive pairing of design with deep research that yields insight into real life.*

- **Design is generative.** It creates articles that we can all look at and think about. Design can model the interface between the system and the customer—that last layer of a system that generates an experience for any person who engages with it. It can create a clear vision of how things could or should be. At Adaptive Path, we're constantly amazed by the amount of great discussion that can arise from a simple sketch. That's why we sometimes run through dozens of sketches for a single point in the experience (Figure 6-3). While working on a prominent news web site, we created sketches of its primary story page, assigning the sketches names like "hamburger"

---

* Malcolm Gladwell, *The Tipping Point*, (Little, Brown and Company, 2002), pp. 122-7.

(a sandwich-style layout) and "world gone mad" (where all assumptions about the layout were reversed). This allowed us to quickly understand and evaluate a wide array of options.

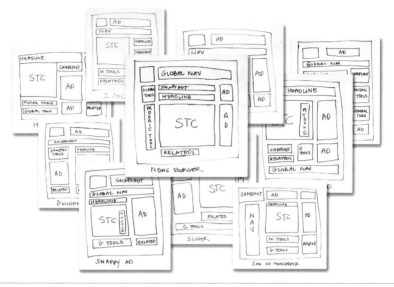

Figure 6-3. A handful of the 300+ sketches generated for one key page of a prominent news site.

- **Design is about making decisions.** It enables a quick exploration of tradeoffs, showing different combinations of components in different orientations. Anyone can see and respond to design, and it can move to a chosen context for evaluation—a home, a store shelf, a factory floor, or an operations center.

To accommodate explorative design, the McDonald's innovation center works out of a warehouse, where entire kitchen and restaurant concepts can be simulated and tested. "It allows us to fail fast so we don't invest in the wrong things," says Denis Weil, Director of Innovation Planning and Advanced Concepts at McDonald's Corporation.* Apple followed a similar line of thought when it developed its retail space. One of the best pieces of advice that Steve Jobs said he received about the space was "go rent a warehouse and build a prototype of a store, and not, you know, just design it, go build 20 of them, then discover [what] didn't work."†

But most organizations don't actively participate in design. It's outsourced, delegated, pushed away. Somehow, design isn't seen as a suitable way to confront and solve problems. Instead, we ineffectually flail at these problems with bulleted slide decks, passionless meetings, and soulless reports.

The Misconceptions of Design

Unfortunately, design is often poorly understood and practiced, and its reputation is only recently catching up with its potential. But while design is making headlines in the business press, the specifics are rarely detailed. And so naturally there are many misconceptions about the practice. The realities are:

- **Design isn't only for designers.** When we discussed research in Chapters 3 and 4, we made it clear that researchers aren't the only sources for research insight. The same holds true for design. At Adaptive Path, we've seen some of the best design decisions come from business leads, marketers, developers, and writers.

- **Design isn't a panacea.** Despite rumors to the contrary, "design thinking" won't solve every last business problem you encounter. You need design thinking, business thinking, operational thinking, and more to help you identify a range of potentially valuable solutions.

- **Design isn't easy.** There are methods for design but no formulas. It often fails, but that's part of how it works. By finding out what doesn't work, you move more quickly toward what does. What's

---

* Aili McConnon, "Want a Master of Design with That?" *BusinessWeek*, October 6, 2006.
† Jerry Useem, "Apple: America's Best Retailer," *Fortune Magazine*, March 8, 2007.

more, because design isn't formulaic, you'll naturally arrive at different outcomes than your competitors, and those outcomes may be better than you ever imagined.

The Potential of Design

Anything elevated to the level of an organizational competency has to align with both the organization's strategy and its system for doing business. Without this business perspective, design fails. Strategy, systems, and design are all innately about tradeoffs. An elegant system can't be weighed down by the complexity of too many parts. A powerful strategy needs tradeoffs to combine differentiation with an effective use of resources—doing some of everything isn't a strategy. Design also forces tradeoffs. There's only so much area on a sheet of paper, space on a screen, room in your pocket, or time for an interaction.

But what's really powerful is how systems, strategy, and design can work together. We talked about Deborah Adler's SafeRx pill bottle as an embodied experience strategy in Chapter 2. When Adler showed that bottle design to Target, it obviously captured the company's imagination. Target recognized that this new bottle could demonstrably differentiate their pharmacy business, win more customers, and effectively become the Volvo of the drug delivery business. Target could have never arrived at this new business plan for its pharmacy through analytical reports on market conditions and sheer deductive business logic. It took Adler's detailed example of a new customer offering to establish a vivid understanding of the kind of pharmacy business Target could become.

The story gets really interesting when you realize that this pill bottle isn't just a physical object, it's actually a system. Target appropriately calls the bottle ClearRX, describing it more broadly as a "prescription distribution and communication system."* That's because it required quite a bit of work on the back end to make the pill bottles work on the front end.

---

* "ClearRX at Target Pharmacy Backgrounder" Target.com Pressroom, January 28, 2007.

So let's just look at one aspect of the pill bottle design—the bottle rings. The concept is simple enough: color-coded rings show customers which bottles are theirs and help prevent them from accidentally taking someone else's prescription. However, the implementation is much more difficult. Target has to ensure that the right color ring goes around the right prescription, so Target's Pharmacy IT system has to track which family member has which color ring, so they don't accidentally switch the colors when they fill the next prescription.

It's clear that considerable design effort went into the processes and systems surrounding the pill bottle. As Adler describes it, it was, "an enormous undertaking…a huge collaborative effort."[*] Here's a hint of the overall system that Adler had to consider:

> *"I work with the pharmacy team, pharmacy operations, the Target technology team to build the software to accommodate the new labeling system, the marketing team… there were major training sessions to train all the pharmacists on how to use this new system because they were the most important people to us. They were the front line. They had to explain how to use this new system, and they had to learn how to use it."*[†]

All this systemic change resulted from a single pill bottle design. Working "backward," from a design artifact to the systems and people that would support it yielded a dramatic increase in business. Target's pharmaceutical drug sales increased an estimated 14 percent the year after the ClearRX was introduced, much more than one suspects it would have if Target had built from the back-end systems forward.[‡]

---

[*] Brian Collins, Deborah Adler. "A Dose of Design: Target's ClearRX" BusinessWeek—Innovation of the Week, BusinessWeek.com podcast, May 9, 2006.

[†] Collins, Adler, ibid.

[‡] "Chain Store Guide Information Services Research Report," MarketResearch.com.

In this case (and many others), design is more than a method for making an offering more appealing and acceptable. The act of design gives form to a powerful idea that many can rally around. Design artifacts can embody strategy, articulate requirements for an entire system, and define clear requirements for a compelling and economically valuable customer experience.

Design Can't Do It Alone

Design can and will fail when it's practiced outside of the context of systems and strategy. Take the airline industry consortium that devised a software application for frequent flyers who book their own travel online. The design was elegant and, as user testing proved, highly usable. But the user testing also proved something else—none of these frequent flyers would use the software application because they were all busy traveling, often without access to a computer or dial-up connectivity. Despite the elegant user interface, the strategy was faulty, and the proposed system would have increased the complexity of travel for the targeted consumer. The sponsoring company killed the project.

When applied well, strategy provides useful boundaries to the design activity. As Charles Eames said of the relationship, "Here is one of the few effective keys to the design problem—the ability of the designer to recognize as many of the constraints as possible—his willingness and enthusiasm for working within these constraints."* Sam Lucente, head of design at HP, has also shared his take on the effectiveness of such constraints:

> *"For the longest time, ideation was about throwing out as many ideas as you can. We've realized pretty quickly it's really not about a bunch of ideas; it's about really good strategy, alignment with business, diag-*

---

* "Films of Charles and Ray Eames, Volume 4," Image Entertainment: Charles and Ray Eames, 1967.

nostics, and deep customer understanding. And when you're ready to talk about ideas, bringing people to the table who are informed is what it's all about." [*]

Design as an Organizational Competency

An organizational competency is a company's integral talent, something that it does well and gives it a competitive edge. An organization might have a competency in running an efficient supply chain (Wal-Mart), creating technological innovations (Bose), or maintaining and strengthening a brand (Disney). Organizations typically have multiple competencies, and strong organizations evolve and coordinate their competencies to synch with customer needs.

For design to become corporate competency, it has to be more than just a department of people with the cool shoes, more than the activity you perform just prior to commercialization. Design is a way of approaching problem solving, decision making, and strategic planning that can yield better outcomes. It's an open approach, and anyone in the organization can participate to generate solutions, make insightful and meaningful decisions, and build empathetic offers that address needs that customers may not even know they have. As markets, lives, and the world become more complex, developing design as a core competency will be a key business practice for small and large companies alike.

Organizational competencies in optimization and efficiency, such as Six Sigma, Total Quality Management, Supply Chain Management, and Business Process Reengineering, have been applied to a point of diminishing returns. In most industries, efficiency has simply become a required capability instead of a competency that differentiates companies from competitors. Both Wal-Mart and Dell were leaders in their industries until Target, Best Buy, HP, and Apple began to apply these same readily available optimization practices. Now it's the retailers

---

* Hindo, Brian. "The Front Lines' of Innovation," *BusinessWeek*, November 2, 2005.

creating differentiated customer experiences that are growing stronger. Organizations have expanded their focuses from costs and their impact on the bottom line to include new ways to grow revenue and the top line.

Rather than trying to repeat earlier successes by doing the same old things more efficiently, a design competency leads an organization toward exploring and imaging new sources of revenue and competitive advantage. Roger Martin, Dean of the Rotman School of Management, explains that design-centric organizations "peer into the needs and desires of their customers, identify patterns of behavior, refine ideas that tap into those behaviors, then push into the unknown—or at least the uncertain."* Unless an organization has differentiated offerings that really address customer needs, there's nothing for a business to hone, measure, or make more efficient.

Embedding Design in the Organization

So, we've established that design isn't a standalone activity, and it's certainly not a strategy unto itself. At Adaptive Path, we look to the other competencies within an organization and combine design with those to generate more effective solutions—for example, design combined with technological experimentation at an entrepreneurial startup, or design and content creation expertise for a media company. Jim Wicks, Vice President and Director of Motorola's Consumer Experience Design, explained that his group began to make headway as they partnered with the marketing group, "woven tightly together" to define future strategies.†

---

* Roger Martin, "Tough Love," *Fast Company*, October 2006, p. 54.

† Jim Wicks and Brandon Schauer, "Perspectives: Weaving Design into Motorola's Fabric," Institute of Design 2006 Strategy Conference web site, May 2006.

These combinations are powerful not just because of the way design can improve other competencies, but also because of how those other competencies can improve design. For example, we let financial analysis drive our design decisions with a financial planning and services firm. Industry "best practices" suggested focusing on supporting transactions, such as buying and selling stocks. Our research showed that our client's customers were fundamentally different from their competitors' customers, and our financial analysis encouraged us to shift toward supporting non-transaction activities like asset tracking and assessment, because these interactions would generate the greatest value for our client. We used a financial lens to break through to a unique design solution.

Through research we conducted on user experience in organizations, we've found that the larger the firm, the more likely it is to have a department responsible for the design of user experiences. Perhaps paradoxically, the larger the firm, the less likely that it has a top-level executive who is responsible for the user experience.

These are troubling observations for growing organizations. When user experience becomes compartmentalized, it's no longer the shared responsibility of everyone within an organization. What would Walt Disney World be like if only some employees felt responsible for hosting a good experience? Experts can facilitate design, but anyone at an organization should feel welcome to participate. The experiences design creates must be everyone's responsibility.

The Mayo Clinic offers an excellent case of embedding design within an organization. This world-renowned medical practice is recognized for its excellence in medical care, research, and education. In 2002, the clinic launched the SPARC program (see, plan, act, refine, communicate), to rapidly experiment with new models of practicing medicine (Figure 6-4). They realized early that they lacked the tools to find and address unmet needs in medical care; their understanding of experimentation wasn't deep enough. So SPARC included designers and worked with external design firms like IDEO to learn and incorporate design methods into the SPARC program.

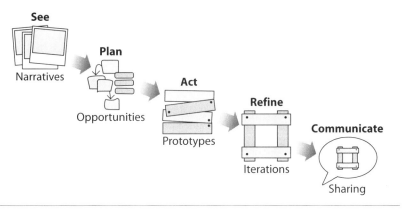

Figure 6-4. The SPARC model.

As a result, SPARC has found interesting ways to combine the generative nature of design with the safety and rigor of medical practice. Alan Duncan, the medical director of SPARC, says that their process, "involves bringing design principles and experimental rigor closer together. When we find something that works in prototype form we always wrap around it the rigor of the experimental design to understand what impact it's going to have on the patient and on the organization—in terms of effectiveness, in terms of quality, and in terms of patient safety."* The result is a program that more effectively creates and shares improvements to the patient-provider relationship.

SPARC also exemplifies an organization overcoming many of the challenges to integrating design as a core competency:

- **Design isn't always intuitive.** SPARC had to extend beyond its initial assumptions that the lab was just about medical experimentations. They had to take on new design processes to make their vision possible.

---

* Dr. Alan K. Duncan, MD and Brandon Schauer. "Persepctives: Innovation Rigor," Institute of Design Strategy Conference web site, May 2005.

- **Qualitative insights are difficult to act upon.** SPARC learned to translate qualitative data into prototypes that allowed users to offer their insights.

- **Design can't do it alone.** As Duncan explains, "We need to bring a marriage between design principles and experimental rigor."

Building a Competitive Competency

Many organizations stand at the threshold of integrating design to a level at which it can become a powerful, competitive competency. First, you have to be aware of the benefits of design relative to existing business practices. You can't build a design competency overnight; it requires difficult changes in processes, skills, and perhaps most importantly, culture.

Once the changes take root, however, an organization can wield its new competency to long-term advantage—harvesting new ideas, making them possible, and then delivering exceptional experiences to an increasingly loyal customer base.

Advantages of a Design Competency

Design, in the right hands, can reach new markets or extend your organization's assets and capabilities. When a business achieves design competency, crafting valuable experiences is easier and more advantageous.

In the Beginning

Development of new products and services begins in a haze. It's never clear where the best ideas will come from or how long it will take to find them, which is why this early stage is often called "the fuzzy front end." You know you're in the fuzzy front end when:

- **Anticipation far exceeds insight.** There's much more interest in what could be developed than wisdom about what should be developed.

- **Plans seem arbitrary.** You can't schedule the creation of brilliant ideas. Any milestones you set are complete guesswork.

- **No amount of research data is enough.** Despite mountains of research data, insights remain elusive.

- **Uncertainty runs rampant.** The set of potential solutions seems endless, especially because the problem can be described in multiple ways.

Most organizations lack the talent to find fresh and marketable ideas in the fuzz, because this stage is poorly understood. Yet every process downstream from the fuzzy front end is shaped and determined by its outcome. Design offers a means of framing your problem, revealing relevant ideas and new paths forward.

Traditional Tools Can't Tame the Fuzz

Product-and-service development is one of the trickiest feats in business. Chicago-based strategy firm Doblin estimates that 96 percent of innovation efforts result in failure.* It's not that businesses don't understand how to market and deliver new products and services, it's that they don't know how to locate the great opportunities and ideas in the fog.

There are many familiar ways to manage and improve the later stages of new product development, but don't expect structured processes such as Stage Gate™ (a formalized and staged process of task completion and review) or Design for Six Sigma to transform marginal ideas into great customer experiences. You first need a means of pulling great ideas out of the fray.

---

* Larry Keeley. Interview with GK VanPatter, "The Business of New," NextDesign Leadership Institute web site. 2003.

Even the masters of these rigorous processes recognize this limitation. Stage Gate pioneer Dr. Robert G. Cooper explains, "Don't expect a well-oiled new product process to make up for a shortage of quality ideas: if the idea was mundane to start with, don't count on your process turning it into a star!"*

Great Execution Isn't the Answer

Great efforts can't transform lame ideas. The "internet appliance," for example, was an idea that many organizations thought they understood—Intel, Compaq, Gateway, Microsoft, and 3Com all took a swing at it. 3Com created Audrey, an elegantly designed interactive tool meant to fit into the kitchen. It was little more than a $499 calendar, address book, and set of preloaded web sites, and almost no one wanted it.

Another example of pulling the wrong idea out of the fuzz is Mobile ESPN, the now-defunct mobile phone service designed to keep fans-on-the-go updated with sporting scores and events (Figure 6-5). After ESPN spent $150 million to become a mobile virtual network operator and launch a phone service, only one-tenth of the necessary customer base signed up for the phone in the months after its launch. *BusinessWeek* contributor Tom Lowry put it best, "At Mobile ESPN's launch, the company said there were plenty of people out there willing to pay for the privilege of getting sports all the time, whether at the grocery store, the kid's soccer game, or waiting for the bus. But even a 19-year-old sports junkie has other avocations, even if they are just sex and beer."†

---

* Robert G. Cooper, Scott J. Edgett, and Elko J. Kleinschmidt, "Optimizing the Stage-Gate˚ Process: What Best-Practice Companies are Doing, Part 1," *Research Technology Management*, September 2002.

† Tom Lowry, "ESPN's Cell-Phone Fumble" BusinessWeek Online, October 30, 2006.

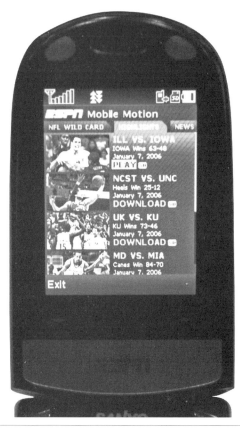

Figure 6-5. Mobile ESPN: an expensive failure.

Examples of failed products and services are all around: Delta's discount Song Airlines, Gap Inc.'s Forth and Town stores, or the Volkswagen Phaeton. Most of these were coupled with respectable design and development efforts. Strong execution simply couldn't overcome the folly of the original ideas.

Getting Started on the Best Path

In a 2007 *Harvard Business Review* article, Jim Hackett, president and CEO of the office furniture manufacturer Steelcase, reviewed past struggles with his own company's fuzzy front end, "Simply put, we made the same mistake that most organizations make when they undertake an ambitious project—having come up with a fine notion, we put all our energy into execution before we had thought the idea through."* Organizations jump to conclusions quickly, applying deductive logic and best practices, but are surprised when they haven't generated something different and better than the competition.

Notions of what to create come easily, and it's worth exploring many of them. Rather than finding one idea and charging forward, it's wise to find a way to look at the haze more systematically so you can choose from many more new ideas. Designers help this process in three key ways:

1. **Presupposing multiple solutions.** Deductive, solid, business thinking often leads to a single conclusion from the facts on hand. Designers are sometimes more open to possibility. They use what Darden professor Jeanne Liedtka calls abductive reasoning, suggesting alternatives based on partial data. Liedtka says the designer "embraces the logic of what might be. Designers may not be able to prove that something 'is' or 'must be,' but they nevertheless reason that it 'may be.'"†

Adaptive Path worked with a provider of corporate retirement plans. Our task was to generate posters that described various potential futures for the company's multi-channel customer experience (Figure 6-6). By looking at many different scenarios for future experience, we were able to improve and evaluate these different futures from the perspectives of the business, the corporate customer, the

---

* James P. Hackett, "Preparing for the Perfect Product Launch", *Harvard Business Review*, April 1, 2007.

† Roger Martin, "Creativity That Goes Deep" *BusinessWeek*, August 3, 2005.

end customer, and the brand. This activity not only helped us find the right future for the company, but the discussions we had with the client revealed components of a solution that the organization found exciting to develop.

Figure 6-6. One of many posters used to evaluate and improve a potential future experience for a financial services firm.

2. **Shifting focus and taking off the blinders.** Organizations and industries are often into looking at problems from perspectives that worked well in the past. A design approach can shift focus from sales to service, or from system to customer, and in the process uncover novel ideas. Changing the questions you ask can also reframe the fuzz. What if the problem with internet appliances isn't about creating the right device, but about creating the right services? Design is about removing blinders and using relevant, readily accessible insights to drive out new ideas and inform the decision-making.[*]

---

[*] Max H. Bazerman, "Decisions Without Blinders" *Harvard Business Review*, January 1, 2006.

At Adaptive Path, we took on a challenge to imagine a better-designed portable insulin pump for the diabetics who use it. By spending time in the lives of actual diabetics, we took off the blinders and found that the issues weren't all medical or logistical in nature. For many, their personal image, or more specifically, a way to hide their pumps was a significant desire. Remaining active and having sex were also big challenges for anyone attached to a pump. And for many diabetics, maintaining a positive outlook and keeping motivated were real factors in staying healthy. By taking off the blinders, the Adaptive Path team reframed the problems from one of medicine to one involving the larger contexts of emotion, lifestyle, and image.

3. **Defining constraints that drive great solutions.** Sometimes constraints trigger great ideas, especially dealing head-on with a constraint that prior solutions—and maybe existing solutions from competitors—have tried to dodge.

   A few quick examples: What if you could send it overnight? (FedEx) What if you could carry all of your music with you? (iPod) What if there were no late fees for video rentals? (Netflix) What if laptops were cheap enough that everyone could have one? (One Laptop Per Child) What if you could watch TV on your own schedule? Tivo.

   Asking the right questions can result in tremendous new experiences, but how do you find the constraints that lead to these questions? First, it takes customer empathy, and knowing what obstacles and shortcomings really drive customers nuts. As a part of customer research, you occasionally witness a moment of clarity from someone struggling through an experience: All I really want to do is… know if I'm saving enough. Or start a blog. Or use my new phone.

   Second, it takes a newbie mindset. Deep familiarity with industries and organizations can lead you to accepting and working around obstacles that could actually be removed with a great new solution. Design methods can help you recognize these obstacles, typically by considering the larger context of the problem.

Adaptive Path has done some work with Soundflavor, a music-search and recommendation service that serves as a companion to software like iTunes (Figure 6-7). From the start, the assumption was that Soundflavor would be both a web site and a desktop application, but by the second day of work, the team asked, "What if we pack the power of an application into the size and utility of a desktop widget?" A prototype developed the same day proved this constraint to be a powerful solution. The simplicity of a widget matched the goal of effortless use, instantaneous creation of playlists, and easy integration with other applications and the Soundflavor web site. As the project developed, the "form" of the software changed greatly, but always had that widget feel. A full application wouldn't have been nearly so successful.

Figure 6-7. Initial vision prototype and the final design of the Soundflavor DJ application.

Flickr Framed

Each of these three approaches—finding multiple solutions, shifting focus, and defining constraints—can reframe the problem space and reveal a pathway out of the fuzz, but they're most powerful when combined. Again, take Flickr as an example. Before creating Flickr, the service's founders first made other attempts at experiences that could support online community. They knew they needed to provide people with "excuses to hang out"* and eventually discovered photo sharing as a promising approach. But rather than simulating offline photo experiences, they realized that they should shed the metaphors of the old print world and embrace an open platform to integrate with camera phones, blogs, and the rest of the Web.

Setting constraints for themselves, which they share via their About Flickr page, is perhaps the most lasting method the Flickr Staff used to emerge from the fuzz. When asked to explain these constraints, Flickr co-founder Caterina Fake said, "I think we sat down and did some soul-searching and wrote down all the reasons and broke them down into clusters and this was what emerged. We needed a way to explain it to people… this is why we have what we have." When asked about the usefulness of constraint, Fake remarked, "It's indispensable. These are the things that will put you on the true path." While Flickr succeeded by setting constraints, rapidly exploring new possibilities can offer a different kind of advantage.

The Idea Lab

A prototype of a clearly desirable experience can have dramatic impact by making an idea actionable and exciting. Design gives form to ideas so that their value can be communicated, evaluated, and improved.

---

* Caterina Fake and Peter Merholz, "MXSF 2007: Interview with Caterina Fake", *AdaptivePath.com* blog, February 12, 2007.

At Adaptive Path, we put aside time twice a week for open design sessions, all-hands meetings where we roll up our sleeves and leave titles and responsibilities at the door. For one hour, everyone in the room—project managers, administrative staff, clients—is a world-class designer. The most successful and engaging of these design sessions focus on translating ideas and insights into design artifacts.

For example, about two dozen of us worked along with a team from a major travel publication to rapidly convert their research findings and rough ideas into multiple sketches of web experiences (Figure 6-8). The magic of the design session for the client team was that we were able to convert a handful of their ideas into tangible solutions that could be further evaluated, improved, or eliminated from contention—and we did it all in just an hour. Traditional methods may have first involved requirements gathering or kept the design work in the hands of just one or two designers rather than a large and diverse group. Those approaches would have taken days or weeks to explore a smaller set of potential solutions.

Figure 6-8. Groups at Adaptive Path's open design sessions quickly convert research findings into concepts for user experiences.

The way design methods can manifest abstract ideas is compelling. With a little practice, your organization can have a high-speed fabrication process for its raw ideas, quickly revealing what works and what doesn't, and, perhaps most importantly, offering a way to learn and move forward to capture extraordinary ideas.

Ideas Are Neither Scarce Nor Fragile

Ideas are cheap, cheap, cheap; we can think of so very many. All too often, though, our organizations treat them as tender, scarce, and special. We detail them meticulously in requirements documents, making sure we completely and fully understand them before we test them.

Ideas live in PowerPoint presentations, where they're treated like descriptions on the sealed box of a toy. Everyone reads the packaging, but dreams up a different idea of the product or experience inside. Most of us don't stop to give form to that great idea in our heads, so we never get to see its true faults and shortcomings. We never get to take what's good about that idea and reincarnate it in the next idea. Good ideas need to fail early and often so you can arrive sooner at a great one. Netflix, for example, uses a "fail fast" approach for steadily improving its site for millions of customers. The lead designer at Netflix says, "We don't assume anything works and we don't like to make predictions without real-world tests. Predictions color our thinking. So, we continually make this up as we go along, keeping what works and throwing away what doesn't. We've found that about 90 percent of it doesn't work."[*]

One of the great fallacies of design and innovation is that great ideas emerge in some smart person's mind and then are immediately translated into a solution. Scott Berkun works to debunk this myth in his book *The Myths of Innovation*. "The dirty little secret—the fact often denied—is that unlike the mythical epiphany, real creation is sloppy.

---

[*] Joshua Porter, "The Freedom of Fast Iterations: How Netflix Designs a Winning Web Site," User Interface Engineering web site, November 14, 2006.

Discovery is messy, exploration is dangerous."* James Dyson has helped to tell a more accurate story of design when telling the story of his Dyson vacuum cleaner (Figure 6-9). It took him 5,127 prototypes to think through the problem and reach the final design.† We need fabricators of ideas to truly understand ideas, see where they fall short, and use tangible forms as a common reference to discuss and decide what will make their products and services better.

Figure 6-9. A Dyson vacuum: the result of thousands of prototypes, failures, and new solutions.

---

* Scott Berkun, *The Myths of Innovation* (O'Reilly Media, Inc., 2007), p. 86.
† James Dyson and Hannah Clark, "James Dyson Cleans Up," Forbes.com, August 1, 2006.

Ideas and Experience Made Manifest With Design

Tim Brown, CEO of product design and innovation firm IDEO, has seen how design artifacts can make strategy more tangible:

> *"Strategy should bring clarity to an organization; it should be a signpost for showing people where you, as their leader, are taking them—and what they need to do to get there.... People need to have a visceral understanding—an image in their minds—of why you've chosen a certain strategy and what you're attempting to create with it.... Because it's pictorial, design describes the world in a way that's not open to many interpretations."*[*]

If product design needs an ounce of pictorial, visceral understanding, the design of experiences needs a metric ton. Few things are more abstract than ideas about experience. Experiences ultimately exist in the minds of customers as subjective perceptions from interactions with an organization.[†] This subjectivity makes experiences difficult to think about, and it makes organizations much less willing to focus on and improve experiences. But a competency in design can turn that around, as Google design manager and Adaptive Path founder Jeffrey Veen notes. He talks about his team at Google designing in real time, "We generally start by filling whiteboards with ideas and potential solutions to the problem we're trying to solve... my favorite phrase in a meeting is, 'You mean like this...?' and someone draws something."[‡]

But sometimes capturing an experience goes deeper than the surface of the whiteboard. Fortunately, you can prototype just about any aspect of an experience: customer service interactions can be scripted and tested, environments can be mocked-up and staged, system interactions can be simulated.

---

[*] Tim Brown, "Strategy by Design," *Fast Company*, June 2005, p. 52.

[†] Christopher Meyer and Andre Schwager, "Understanding Customer Experience", *Harvard Business Review*, February 2007.

[‡] "Fireside Chat with Khoi Vinh and Jeffrey Veen: In-house vs. on your own," Signal vs. Noise weblog, 37signal.com, July 18, 2006.

For example, Adaptive Path was working on the design of an experience that led customers across multiple channels, including retail, web, and phone. We needed to understand what the multi-channel experience might be like, so we created a storyboard to narrate how the various channels and touchpoints could come together to make an experience (Figure 6-10).

Even with a low-resolution linear story, you can begin to understand what's working, what isn't, and where the great ideas lie. You can also springboard interesting discussion about feasibility, scope of the solution, and what's really going to have to happen between any two frames of that simple storyboard.

Figure 6-10. A storyboard makes the story of a new potential user experience more tangible and therefore easy to evaluate and improve.

The Power of Tangible Ideas

As we've mentioned, making ideas tangible lets you play with them and make them better, but prototyping alone isn't the answer. Often prototypes simply end up documenting what the developers already know, offering no insight into the ugly unknowns. But the beauty of prototypes is that they don't have to represent all aspects of the final design; it's possible to prototype only the components or characteristics that you need to better understand. Prototype what you don't know, and then experiment your way to the answer.

Is the experience of buying a car online acceptable to potential car buyers? That's the question IdeaLab! asked before launching the Cars-Direct site in 2001. They answered that question "by building a simple web site, hiring a CEO for 90 days, and charging him with selling one car. The site got 1,000 hits the first day and sold four cars."* In the process, the 90-day CEO had to create each part of the experience at a sufficient level of fidelity to pull off trial: a web site, product profiles, customer service, transactional systems, and delivery. This generative activity may have not been termed "experience design" or "experience prototyping," but that's what it was. The result was a successful prototype; it confronted the business and experience unknowns head-on and produced a clear answer.

Strategy is about choosing in which small set of activities and capabilities your organization should invest so that the resulting offerings create a sustainable advantage. Prototyping at the intersection between your organization's capabilities and customers' lives lets you model an experience that customers will love, then plan backward through organizational processes and operations to figure out how that experience can be delivered.

---

* Andrew Hargadon and Robert I. Sutton, "Building an Innovation Factory," *Harvard Business Review*, May-June 2000, pages 157-166.

Remember these stories where prototyping the interface led to great organizational changes?

- Deborah Adler prototyped a superior pill-bottle design that conveyed new processes and capabilities for the Target pharmacy.

- Apple prototyped multiple versions of its retail store to discover what would and wouldn't work.

Prototypes like these reveal requirements for the experience, both from the customer's perspective, or the "front of the house," and from the organization's perspective, or the "back of the house."* The interface between these perspectives is an ideal point for the people designing to come together and build solutions that are more powerful than either could have created on their own.

Fabricating ideas makes them plainly visible and accessible to evaluation, improvement, and delivery. But planning a system for finding and deploying ideas can take an organization to the next level.

Creating the Long "Wow!"

Businesses have begun to realize that the lofty goal of customer satisfaction might be a red herring. A satisfied customer isn't necessarily a loyal customer; today's satisfied customer might find even more satisfaction in your competitor's offerings tomorrow. And so we've started to see the rapid diffusion of tools like the NetPromoter™ Score, which try to quantify loyalty. Such measures are popular because they track behaviors that create economic value: a customer recommending your brand to a friend, or a customer returning to buy from you again. But measuring loyalty doesn't create loyalty.

---

* Robert J. Glushko and Lindsay Tabas, "Bridging the 'Front Stage' and 'Back Stage,'" *Service System Design*, University of California, Berkeley, School of Information, June 15, 2007.

Loyalty Can't Be Manufactured

It's no surprise that the MBA knee-jerk reaction to the loyalty problem is to create a loyalty program, but you can't manufacture loyal customers by issuing them ID cards. Instead, these artificial attempts at loyalty create extra overhead in the customer relationship, they deliver pseudo-benefits the customer never needed, and they may eventually create customer barriers, resentment, or revolt.

At Adaptive Path, we've observed the superficial nature of loyalty programs first-hand. We talked to customers of a well-known financial institution who were enrolled in a loyalty program. We found multi-millionaire, "platinum-level" customers who didn't know (and didn't care!) about their special status and benefits, even though the company considered that program an essential advantage and an attractor. The customers simply wanted the good products and services they were paying for in the first place.

Customer loyalty can't be bought or bottled. Loyalty grows within people, based on a series of notable interactions they have with products, services, and companies. No card-carrying programs are necessary: Apple doesn't have a traditional loyalty program, and neither does Nike or Harley-Davidson. These companies impress, please, and stand out in the minds of their customers through repeated, notably great experiences.

"Wow!" Engenders Loyalty

Notably great experiences are punctuated by a moment of "Wow!," when the product or service delights, anticipates the needs of, or pleasantly surprises a customer. OXO's Good Grips Angled Measuring Cup (Figure 6-11) triggers such a moment of "Wow!." A set of angled markings on the OXO cup lets you quickly measure liquids for recipes without having to stop cooking and bend over. Suddenly a little part of your life is easier, because OXO thought carefully about the way you cook. This delightful surprise resonates because it feels tailored to your needs.

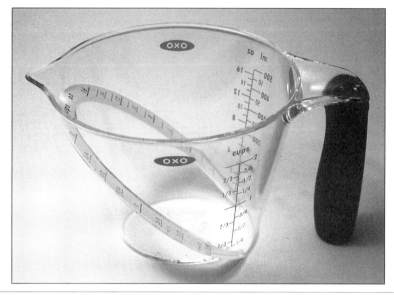

Figure 6-11. OXO's Good Grips Angled Measuring Cup: a surprising improvement on the standard model.

OXO and its partner Smart Design were driven by empathy for their customer. Designers learn empathy by spending time in the lives and environments of real customers, then simulating the experiences that people will have with new offerings through prototyping.

By going deep into customers' lives and closely observing their behaviors, you can wow them when you address needs that they'd never be able to articulate. By immersing yourself in the customer's wider world of emotion and culture, you can wow them by attuning the offering to practical needs and dimensions of delight that normally go unfulfilled.

When a company uses empathetic design methods to create moments of "Wow!" over and over again, it bonds with customers at a level far beyond the realm of gold-colored plastic cards. OXO introduces over 50 products every year, wowing customers with purposeful improvements through the re-imagination of common culinary tools.

Few companies consistently translate rich insights from their customers' lives into better offerings. The few that do can achieve a Long "Wow!," building a true, deep loyalty that transcends traditional loyalty programs.

After the announcement of the Apple iPhone, it was uncanny how often the same words came up in conversations with employees from competing phone manufacturers and mobile network operators. Their response to questions about the iPhone was practically identical, "We're not that worried about the iPhone. We're worried about what comes next." Apple has a reputation for not only releasing good products, but for making repeated releases that keep customers engaged and push market boundaries. Apple's Long "Wow!" is exciting if you're a customer, but worrisome if you're a competitor.

You can achieve long-term customer loyalty by systematically impressing your customers. Go beyond just measuring loyalty, and begin to actively create it.

Four Steps to Your Long "Wow!"

The art of the Long "Wow!" is finding and managing a system that fosters a deeper relationship with customers. Here's how it's done:

1. **Know your platform for delivery.** Recognize the palette of touchpoints that you can combine to deliver "Wow!" experiences. Select a small set of touchpoints across channels that can a) be coordinated to demonstrate your capability to meet a customer's needs, and b) be remixed to deliver new solutions to customers as you define them.

The Nike + iPod Sports Kit combines a pedometer, iPod, and web site to deliver an entirely new running experience that includes spoken feedback on your run, one-button access to "power songs," and the ability to visualize recent runs. You can easily imagine the delivery of future "Wow!" experiences with this set of touchpoints, such as the selection of songs based on your running pace.

2. **Tackle a wide area of unmet customer needs.** Find an area of the customer experience that your organization is passionate about, and has a competitive advantage in understanding or delivering on. It should be an area big enough that you can return to it repeatedly for new insights and opportunities. This is an opportunity to identify some new green space or to re-invent an old space long overlooked by everyone else.

OXO wasn't scared away from kitchen tools just because these items had looked and functioned the same way for decades. Instead, they passionately believed that kitchen tools should work for everyone—including the founder's wife whose arthritis originally inspired the venture. Therefore, OXO focuses on universal design, or "the concept of designing products that are easy to use for the largest possible spectrum of users."*

3. **Create and evolve your repeatable process**. Discover your organization's approach to delivering "Wow!" moments regularly. Start with the process strengths the organization already has—which could be in competencies such as cost/benefit analysis, quality management, or market testing—and blend them with methods of research and prototyping that focus on experience. At Adaptive Path, we like to use video and storyboard prototyping to focus on the impact of experience, rather than the usability of the interface.

---

* OXO, "Who We Are," www.oxo.com

These methods demonstrate how the experience potentially brings something compelling to the life of the customer and where the "Wow!" happens.

Blending two seemingly disparate processes can be quite powerful. The previously referenced Mayo Clinic's SPARC program mixes the rigor of medical experimental testing with the speed of designing through prototypes to transform the way healthcare services are delivered to patients. The reliability of existing process strengths, like randomized controlled trials, creates repeatability of more qualitative methods for re-imagining patient experiences.

4. **Plan and stage the "Wow!" experiences.** Developing all your ideas at once is risky. Instead, organize a pipeline of "Wow!" moments that can be introduced through your platform of touchpoints over the long haul. As you learn more about your customers and how they perceive the "Wow!" moments, you can better organize your pipeline of ideas for development. Outline where and when additional "Wow!" experiences will emerge, unfolding in a coordinated network of experiences.

Introducing the right experience at the right place and the right time can delightfully surprise customers. WeightWatchers coordinated a platform of meetings, plans, books, and web-based tools to support weight loss. However, WeightWatchers participants probably aren't eating at meetings or in front of computers where they can access the web site. So WeightWatchers released an On-The-Go application for mobile devices (Figure 6-12). It helps plan and track your diet wherever you go, then synchronizes with your diet plan and the web application.

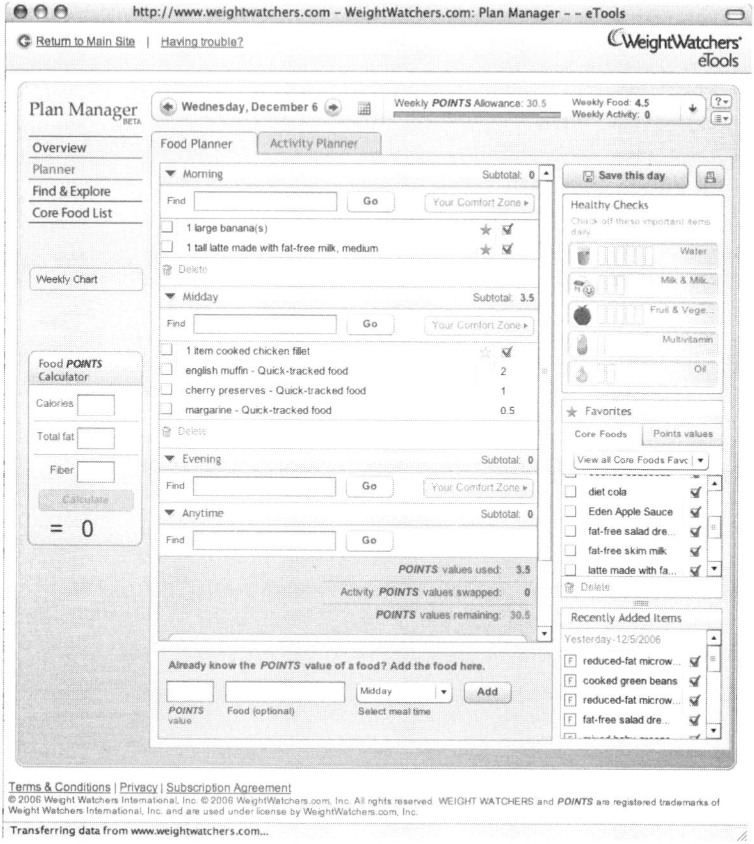

Figure 6-12. WeightWatchers' On-The-Go application for mobile devices.

Relinquishing Control

Hopefully this chapter hasn't given you the impression that by designing experiences, you are somehow controlling experiences. Experiences are determined by the mind and will of the people with whom you're interacting. When you try to control the interaction and tightly manipulate the outcome of the experience, customers tend to rebel.

Think of how the music recording industry has tried to tightly control the format, distribution, and cost of music. As soon as digital music offered a different alternative, people abandoned the old channel in droves. Natalia Davis of investing and advising firm Kairos, Inc. calls this condition "resentful bondage." She explains, "When customers are held hostage by barriers to exit that are too high, deep resentment and anger sets in. This can lead to a revolt!"* Blockbuster had a tight hold on the video rental market in the U.S., making profits by charging customers for holding onto their videos for too long. Once Netflix offered the alternative of keeping a video as long as you wanted, many customers switched to this more flexible system.

Control Is Shortsighted

A similar story played out in online search. In the days before Google, search engines like Excite, Hotbot, and Altavista larded themselves up with content in a desperate effort to hold users beyond the two pages of a search activity: the search box page and the results page. The goal was "stickiness," discouraging people from leaving your domain. When Google launched, one reason it shocked the Web community was its focus on sending you directly to where you actually wanted to go. How could there be a successful business model in actively sending people away from your site? Seven years and a $155 billion market capitalization later, that question has obviously been answered. The other search engines attempted to control your behavior. Google recognized that users maintain control, and to win they had to become the users' preferred choice.

---

* Natalia Davis, Russell Redenbaugh, and Brandon Schauer, "Perspectives: Value: Know It, See It, Design For It," ITT Institute of Design 2006 Strategy Conference web site, May 2006.

Control Limits Growth

Control assumes a more centralized and top-down approach to design, where decisions rest in the hands of a few. With fewer hands and fewer minds, you obviously get fewer new ideas. Good ideas often go undeveloped when they have to make it up a corporate hierarchy before getting a green light.

Historically, McDonald's is an example of a big top-down organization with a very regimented "quality formula" for how to run every restaurant. It took an individual on the front line to buck the regimented corporate system and invent the drive-thru, a huge moneymaker for McDonald's that essentially doubles a restaurant's mealtime volume. The inventor of the drive-thru was a McDonald's franchise owner who just wanted a way to sell more burgers at lunch and (literally) knocked down a wall to make it happen. Had McDonald's supported new ideas from the field, how many other new services might have they discovered? Present pragmatic people with a need and an opportunity, and they can show you how to grow your business.

When an organization is too tight with its control, it stifles growth. In the late 1990s, CNN.com was targeted by users who would "wrap" CNN's content within another site—i.e., embedding a CNN news page within a second site. CNN's responded to having their content confiscated this way by instructing their lawyers to send cease and desist letters to offending sites. More recently, YouTube and other web-based services have propagated themselves into popularity by taking the opposite approach. They make their content easy to embed into any web page that will have them.

DIY Design: The Customer as Designer

Luckily, design is a competency that can be developed both inside and outside of an organization by working with partners and customers that stretch beyond the typical borders of the organization. When an organization has built the ability to reframe its challenges and quickly fabricate ideas, it's then able to consider relinquishing control to customers as core participants in the design process. Customers can create, vet, and extend ideas that will help to shape an organization's future offerings.

Again and again, the history of the Web shows us the value of relinquishing control. Google, Amazon, and eBay have all made their Application Programming Interfaces (APIs) available to the public, where they've evolved in all kinds of unforeseen and innovative ways. For example, developer Paul Rademacher used the API for Google Maps and Craigslist to create his HousingMaps service that geographically maps the locations of apartment rental listings from Craigslist (Figure 6-13). The API for Google Maps is also used with data from the Chicago Police Department to show the location of recent crimes (Figure 6-14). Sometimes these extensions just broaden the reach of a web service, and sometimes they lead to new experiences and capabilities, which are in turn folded back into the original design. Everybody wins, the original creators of the API, the new adapters of the API, and the customers themselves.

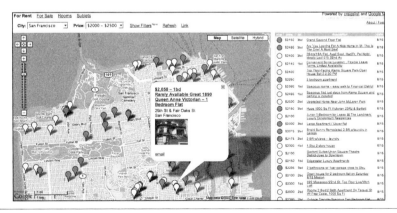

Figure 6-13. HousingMaps integrates Google Maps and Craigslist, allowing users to review apartment lists geographically.

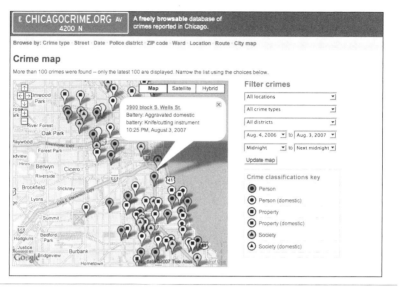

Figure 6-14. Google Maps is integrated with crime reports of the Chicago Police Department to allow users to see the most relevant crimes—the ones close to them.

While organizations that open up APIs encourage customers to design at the fringes of the web service, others make it their mainstay. Online t-shirt store Threadless accepts t-shirt designs submitted by members, then only manufactures and sells those that the site's community has voted as desirable.

The power of relinquishing control can also be found in the offline world. Puma's Mongolian Shoe BBQ (a cute reference to American Chinese buffet restaurants) is set up in participating retail stores where you can create the perfect shoe design by assembling a number of possible sub-components. Just a few weeks later, your custom-designed shoe is delivered to your door. Beyond the profits of selling this customized shoe, imagine the valuable patterns of customer data that this mass customization provides for Puma.

Giving your customers tools to be designers lets you explore options that you may never think of or invest in on your own. Suddenly your design and development team expands from the tens to the thousands.

Design Competency: A Strategic Advantage

As we've learned, design competency can allow an organization to create and sustain a competitive advantage over its rivals by providing an understanding of customers and showing how best to deliver ideal solutions for them. In most markets, a company's cost advantage or technology advantage can be temporary, but the ability to reframe possibilities and translate new ideas into great experiences again and again gives companies a sustained leadership in the market.

In the next chapter, we'll discuss powerful lightweight processes that allow you to deliver great products and services in the future. As Peter Drucker, the creator of modern business management, so plainly put it, "the best way to predict the future is to create it."

CHAPTER 7

The Agile Approach

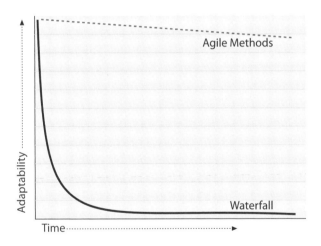

In an environment where exploration leading to a dead end is viewed as an expense to be reduced, true innovation is difficult.

As you have seen, developing products and services for markets in this context is challenging, to say the least. Fortunately there are approaches that make success more likely, even in this environment. Some of these approaches are "new" in the sense that they are gaining increased visibility and popularity, although their antecedents go back many years. The approaches are inspired in part by the collection of development methodologies that fit under the umbrella of "Agile Development," as well as a return to some earlier development methods. One thing they have in common is that the methods all point to the importance of fast prototyping and rapid iteration cycles.

The Agile Manifesto

In early 2001, a group of practitioners of various software development approaches that were at the time referred to as "light" methodologies met informally in Utah. While they did not care for the label "light," the term was used to distinguish their approaches from the heavyweight alternatives then popular for large development projects and in big corporations. Although they were grouped together under a common descriptive umbrella, there was great diversity among their practices. In spite of, or perhaps because of this diversity, the developers were interested in discovering common threads in their work. The search resulted in the creation of the Agile Manifesto:

Individuals and interactions	over	processes and tools
Working software	over	comprehensive documentation
Customer collaboration	over	contract negotiation
Responding to change	over	following a plan

That is, while we acknowledge that there is value in the items on the right, we value the items on the left more.

It is important to note that the Agile Manifesto is a distinct philosophy rather than a specific methodology or set of techniques. While various Agile methods implement this philosophy in different ways, they are all driven by the same underlying values.

Less than Agile: The Waterfall Approach

At the simplest level, many of the Agile approaches emerged in reaction to the waterfall model of software development. The waterfall model, as commonly understood and implemented, is a strictly sequential process of multiple stages moving irreversibly from one to the next (Figure 7-1). Starting from an initial stage that establishes complete requirements, it proceeds to design, implementation, and finally, testing and launch. Each of these stages stands in isolation, with all of the work complete before the next stage begins. This model, one with which we are all quite familiar, seems logical at the outset; it has an appealing simplicity and provides us with a sense that we are in control.

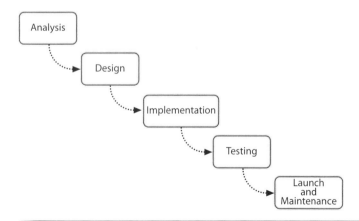

Figure 7-1. The Waterfall approach is so named because all work and information flows downhill from one stage to the next.

It's easy to draw parallels between the waterfall approach as applied to software development and methods successfully applied to production lines. On the surface, the waterfall model appears to scale easily. Because only one task or type of work is attempted at a time, we get the sense that we can avoid complexity and confusion. From a business planning perspective, it also has a clear advantage in that it seems more predictable and amenable to specific timelines, feature lists, and launch dates. It is exactly these types of predictions and plans that seem to be required by our job descriptions. Unfortunately, like many other tidy approaches to complex problems, the waterfall method tends to collapse, sometimes dramatically, in the face of changing conditions.

The irony is that the "never look back" waterfall model was originally about iteration. Winston Royce, who introduced the waterfall model in a 1970 article titled "Managing the Development of Large Software Systems," clearly called for least two cycles of iteration.[*] The truth is that most software development addresses complex requirements and needs exploratory programming or some level of experimentation to get to the appropriate solution. This is true even in the rare cases when the underlying problem remains stable during the entire development process. More commonly however, development aims at a moving target. Markets change, strategies shift, or goals are reevaluated. And the classic waterfall method, which asks for an ironclad design up front before all of the factors can be considered adequately, is rarely up to the task.

But the flaws of the waterfall method run even deeper. The fundamental problem is that it's often impossible to accurately articulate all of a project's needs up front, and trying to anticipate all of the eventual requirements a year or two ahead of time is daunting, if not impossible. So, it's no surprise that when we use the waterfall method, we sometimes arrive at a project's final deliverable only to discover "new" critical needs

---

[*] Winston Royce, "Managing the Development of Large Software Systems." *Proceedings of IEEE WESCON* (August 1970), pp.1-9.

or features that must be implemented. There is no room in the waterfall process for reacting to new information, whether the information emerges from problems that arise during development, user feedback based on actual use, or changes in the market.

In some cases, finding developers with deep experience in a particular domain can alleviate some of these risks. A developer who has built 20 different content-management systems knows the types of issues that are likely to come up on the 21st project. Having that kind of experience available during the initial design phase can be priceless, but it can be tough to find those experts. In addition, purely external forces may spawn new requirements during the development process. New market developments may invalidate earlier decisions; no amount of expertise can alleviate that impact.

In actual practice, even proponents and practitioners of the waterfall model tend to tweak the process to allow for some feedback and interaction between stages. In an attempt to shoehorn some flexibility into a project, we've seen a variety of approaches that allow organizations to feel that they are still sticking with the letter of the "organized" waterfall method but still permit some looseness around the edges. The rigid stages sometimes overlap, either by sharing personnel or delaying the end of one stage until the succeeding stage has begun. However, the advantages of allowing stages to "leak" are limited. This kind of compensatory feedback can only go back or forward one stage; it simply cannot match the flexibility and responsiveness afforded to us by a system designed to be iterative from the start.

The Emergence of Lean Manufacturing

The shortcomings of the waterfall method were part of the impetus for developers to create a new model. In the search for alternatives, Lean Manufacturing, a system developed at Toyota in post-war Japan, was a source of inspiration. In that production environment, consumer demand was low, and a strategy based on reducing unit costs and creating economies of scale wasn't proving to be effective. Reducing waste became a new focus. There were the obvious techniques (e.g., reducing inefficient manufacturing processes and wasted effort), but several more unexpected methods were developed that were equally effective. One of these was to shift from using sales forecasts to drive production schedules and instead let actual consumer demand drive production. Cars were not built in advance, but rather once an order was placed. This required establishing an extremely tight feedback loop between what was actually sold and the production line. The payoff was reduced overproduction and transportation costs. Over time, the responsiveness this engendered expanded to the entire production cycle.

The Agile Approach

As with Toyota's Lean Manufacturing model, the Agile approach embraces some specific tactics for creating a more efficient and cost-effective development process:

- **Highly iterative processes**, with development cycles that tend to be short and quickly adapt to meet needs that become visible only through the course of development.

- **Bringing the customer into the development process**.

- **Creating smaller workgroups** with highly skilled workers who mentor the more junior members of the team.

- **Valuing getting things right,** or right enough, early on, and not allowing fundamental errors or inefficiencies to linger or recur. This is clearly reflected in the Agile emphasis on testing, consistent and thorough peer review, and repeated refactoring.

In addition, Agile development methods attempt to harness, or at least allow for, the unpredictable (Figure 7-2). Imperfect knowledge is a hurdle in both product development and software development. While market forecasting can be remarkably accurate in some cases, you can't depend on it to be reliable. This is increasingly problematic as you attempt to keep up with the developments in the marketplace we've discussed in previous chapters. As you expand our vision of your customer's needs, it's increasingly clear that those needs can be quite complex. Or perhaps more accurately, to keep the solutions for your customers simple, the solutions may be complex for you. Even in cases where the solution itself is not complex, the road you take to reach that solution may not be a well-worn path. For a product or service to succeed in this environment, you must embrace inevitable uncertainties. Agile-inspired development is the answer.

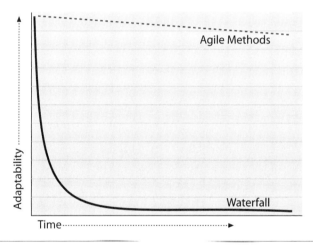

Figure 7-2. In contrast to the Waterfall model, Agile-inspired approaches maintain adaptability throughout a project's lifecycle, not just an early design phase.

Benefits of the Agile Approach

Because Agile processes are so iterative and responsive, exploration is cheaper. This is important: one of the distinct elements of development, especially innovative development in the current environment, is that old answers or approaches may not work. We must explore new approaches with the understanding that many of them will lead to dead ends. In traditional development, one might think of these mistakes as errors rather than understood as useful discoveries. This is understandable in a scenario where somebody makes a best guess at how to tackle a problem and everybody sticks to it. None of us wants to admit a year into a project that a fundamental part of the approach is flawed, and yet it happens all the time. The results are scrapped work, budget problems, and an overdue project—and that's if your team manages to finish it at all.

Lower costs

It's important to have freedom to explore potential solutions without getting tangled in commitments to solutions that prove to be unworkable. With Agile methods, both feedback from customers and the lessons learned from active exploration are consistently evaluated and acted upon. As a result, exploration is both more attractive and less expensive, because true errors in this environment become apparent early in the process, before a big financial investment has been made.

Less documentation

Agile-inspired methods also reduce some of the time and resource-consuming byproducts of development, both by explicit intent and as a fortunate side effect. This is immediately apparent as a great reduction in documentation. This is such an important core principle that it's explicitly stated in the Agile Manifesto. After all, documentation takes resources, and our goal is to build the best product, not to create a perfect set of documents. In the waterfall process, where each stage must stand alone, all communication between teams working on the different stages must occur via documentation. The design stage, for example, produces a design specification consisting of elements such as use cases or feature descriptions; the resulting documents are almost unavoidably huge. By contrast, Agile methods produce relatively little paperwork. Because the design and development processes are intermingled, communication can take place between people in the same room or, more commonly, via an actual working prototype.

Taking the Leap

Drastically reducing documentation like this can feel intimidating, like stepping off a cliff. Instantly our internal voices start saying, "But what if some vague and unnamed emergency happens?" "How will we know what we have done?" "How will we show what we have done?" When this topic is brought up in process discussions there is often a very strong, knee-jerk reaction. But looking back over the past five years, for example, how big is the gap between the pages of documentation that you have created and the pages that were actually used or even looked at a second time?

Fortunately, as this is a practice you can start incrementally, you don't have to jump off a cliff to implement it. Start by surveying the amount of documentation that gets created in your processes, then ask yourself how much of it is truly necessary. Even in cases where you can't eliminate documentation, you can often reduce the "perfection" of the documentation and still reap the benefits of reduced effort. If you really do need 150 wireframes, do they really have to be 150 high-fidelity wireframes or can you get everything we need from 10 high-fidelity and 140 low-fidelity wireframes?

Essential-Only Feature Sets

Agile-inspired approaches also aim to reduce the development of features that are never implemented. This is a common problem in heavier design approaches. Features often make their way into the specification for a product, although they're ultimately unnecessary. It's understandable; we know in these situations that the only way to get a feature we may need into the product is at the very beginning, because the process is stacked so heavily against adding features later. As the development process continues, a feature that turns out to be extraneous is still rolled into the final product because it's listed in the feature specification, and nobody has the authority to remove it or the initiative to question the original decision. Often, even if we proposed the feature and later realize it's no longer needed, we can't remove it, because the process has more authority than we do.

By comparison, the Agile approach continues to incorporate user feedback and continually keeps design open. Unnecessary features can fall away or may even fall away and then be added back in. Because Agile methods support changing direction, hours and resources are not wasted on superfluous features, and the cost of being "wrong" early on is minimal.

Hitting the Sweet Spot—and the Window

Just as with software projects, a first attempt made by a handful of people—or even a larger team—to define a product can only produce an educated guess. Even if it's based on expertise, the resulting solution is likely to be off by just enough to have a significant impact on your profitability or the value you can provide to your customers. Another common problem for product development is that implementation cycles are often so long that the market changes during the course of development. As we've seen, the highly iterative approaches embraced by Agile are designed to incorporate this evolution into ongoing development.

The Iterative Approach: A Little History

Because the Agile approach is so adept at dealing with the new blend of products and services, it's become a popular choice in recent years. However, even though this recently popularity makes the approach feel new, the ideas behind it have been around for some time. NASA's X-15 project from the 1960s, arguably the most successful experimental aircraft in American aviation history, was developed with iterative and incremental delivery. That experience, due to overlapping personnel, led NASA to use a similar approach for the Mercury systems software. They employed time boxes as short as half a day. Even IBM's development of the command-and-control system for the Trident submarine, an extremely large defense project dating back to 1972, used this approach. The best, most consistent, and long-running manifestation of many of these ideas is evident in Lockheed's famed Skunk Works. The facility has turned out cutting-edge products for decades, including the U-2 and the SR-71 Blackbird, using approaches that would seem familiar to any Agile developer.

In addition to having a long track record, the use of the iterative approach is also more widespread even in recent history than commonly supposed. Hewlett-Packard used a similar tactic to develop several innovative products. Engineers would build a prototype and leave it lying around in the open for others to discuss. Feedback was encouraged, some of which might lead nowhere and some of which might lead to a new product.

How Companies Create Agile Environments

In any case, even when feedback was negative or not encouraging, exploration itself was always encouraged. More explicitly, *tangible* exploration was encouraged, a critical point to consider. So, what can you do in your work environment to support this kind of exploration from your most passionate and curious people and not penalize them for the time involved or for discovering dead ends? And once you've taken the first steps, how can you get others inspired as well?

Marching to a Different Drummer

An interesting caveat from HP's history—team evaluation isn't always accurate. An engineer named Chuck House developed an oscilloscope for HP, and David Packard explicitly told him to stop development. Stubbornly, House took vacation time and went across the country getting orders for his product before it existed. Confronted with actual sales, HP put the oscilloscope into production. House later received an award for "extraordinary contempt and defiance beyond the normal call of engineering." While this was an exception to the general rule, this story from HP's history is certainly indicative of a unique corporate culture.

3M: Make a Little, Sell a Little

One company that took an iterative approach is 3M, with its motto, "Make a little, sell a little." As we saw in Chapter 6, 3M has recently started to chase optimization to the exclusion of innovation. Prior to that, however, 3M had a tremendous track record with sales from recently developed products. Not only did 3M have an iterative product development process, it also had business structures in place that let them approach the market incrementally. They could finance a product in stages, and thus reduce the risk associated with potentially unsuccessful products. The company, by this process, also involved consumers directly in production decisions. If a product was an early failure in the marketplace, it didn't pass the gate of consumer acceptance. Of course, one potential drawback with this approach, if you undertake it, is that it can be difficult to scale up quickly enough. Given a choice of problems, however, "too much demand" is a good one to have.

Toyota: Fewer Engineers, Less Development Time

Toyota offers an excellent example of the Agile method as applied to product development. As we mentioned earlier, many of the canonical Lean Manufacturing methods were developed at Toyota. But what sets Toyota apart is not only its production methods but also, just as critically, its product development process. Applying principles derived from Lean Manufacturing further up the process into actual product development allows Toyota to consistently excel in time to market and initial product quality. In comparison to its North American competitors, Toyota uses 25 percent fewer engineers on a vehicle project, and half the development time. All of this, and their end product boasts one of the highest initial quality records in the automotive industry. Their methodology involves exploring alternative approaches early in the development process, maintaining user concerns as a polestar, and providing consistent technical management from start to finish. They also encourage their engineers to stick close to the engineering process, whether that means visiting production lines or building the actual prototypes themselves. These are all familiar approaches to Agile adherents, and the results are clearly exemplary.

The Shifting Landscape: Embedded and Networked Systems

Historical precedents aside, several additional trends push development even further in the Agile direction. These trends not only require more iterative approaches to be successful, but also provide new, more effective methods as part of the iterative toolbox. The first of these is the spread of embedded and networked systems.

Embedded systems are nothing new. They already exist in countless appliances and pieces of consumer electronics. Your microwave, DVD player, iPod, and many other household devices all have microprocessors with various degrees of complexity. As a result, part of their functionality is driven not by hardware but by software. As this approach becomes less and less expensive, there is a drastic and sustained increase in the use of both hardware and software embedded in products. Along with this increased market penetration, the capability of these embedded systems is also growing.

Things get even more interesting when these devices and products can access a network or the world at large. With network access, code that controls these devices can be updated over time, potentially altering their behavior. Updates can occur long after a product's initial sale. Alternatively, a device can behave differently depending on conditions, or can communicate with other devices. Despite development that crosses both department and corporate boundaries, it still provides a cohesive product experience for the consumer. Aside from the larger constella tion of issues that arise when two companies work together, this trend also sparks pure design challenges and questions that the inflexible waterfall approach simply does not allow during product development.

A wonderful example of this is the Nike + iPod Sport Kit, jointly developed by Nike and Apple. A sensor in a pair of running shoes "talks" with the iPod, allowing for a whole new type of product. You can receive workout progress updates through your iPod headphones while you run, and upload the results of your workout for later evaluation.

You'll find another, perhaps more familiar, example of this divide if you compare a VCR and a TiVo. A VCR, once purchased, is a static device. It comes with a certain set of capabilities, and it retains only those capabilities until it breaks down or videotapes become obsolete. From the manufacturer's perspective, there is a clear product development cycle and, while there may be some minor variations over time, the lifecycle is clear and unambiguous. If they want to launch a new product, the company may be able to reuse some of their current technology, but basically, product development starts over from the beginning. A TiVo device, on the other hand, is a platform. The TiVo you buy today may have a whole new range of functionality by next year. Conversely, it's also possible that some functionality could be removed. Regardless, TiVo developers can continue to produce features and functionality without being required to develop, launch, and sell new hardware. This promotes a wonderful new freedom and flexibility.

From a product development perspective, this flexibility can mandate entirely different approaches. First, you have to focus on developing a platform as much as developing an actual product offering. There are some fantastic opportunities here. Perhaps, despite incorporating user feedback in your development process, you're still uncertain about the success of a new set of features. Potentially you could roll out these new features specifically to a small set of users for direct feedback. Or maybe you want to tailor your offerings to certain user segments, so you might provide different features to different users by subscription. It also changes the traditional product-maintenance window. No longer is the scenario simply a single launch followed by product maintenance and support. Now you can have ongoing product development, which implies a much more ambiguous product development cycle. An iterative process with multiple, well-tested, small releases is a much better fit in this context.

MIT's Fab Lab

Another clear and interesting trend is the ongoing developments in rapid prototyping technology and the resulting decrease in equipment costs. MIT's Fab Lab is perhaps the best-known example. Fab Lab is an abbreviation for Fabrication Laboratory, developed at MIT's Center for Bits and Atoms. It's a bundle of off-the-shelf, industrial-grade fabrication and electronics tools, wrapped in open source software and custom programs written by researchers at the Center for Bits and Atoms, and used to create product prototypes. Not too many years ago, a version of the Fab Lab cost $40,000. Today, one can be built for $20,000. In the foreseeable future, this will fall to $10,000, then $5,000 and less. Kelly Johnson, the head of Lockheed's Skunk Works, said, "An engineer should never be more than a stone's throw away from the physical product."* Even now, many companies and research departments have invested in Fab Labs (or the equivalent) of their own, and are starting to achieve greater prototyping capability. Fab Labs are also an increasing presence in educational settings; as a result, there will be a generation of engineers and designers who come of age in an environment where this kind of rapid prototyping is taken for granted. The ability to create physical prototypes quickly and easily is tremendously important for the future of product development.

---

* James Morgan and Jeffrey Liker, "The Toyota Product Development System: Integrating People, Process and Technology," (Productivity Press) 2006. p. 174.

Overcoming Obstacles

Despite clear benefits in the current context, the Agile approach isn't without challenges. Sometimes these challenges are purely institutional. In a large manufacturing firm, the group responsible for new product development may be required to be profitable as a department. While this makes sense from a strictly business perspective, an unfortunate side effect is that it inspires an aversion to error that can be detrimental to Agile development methods. Remember, the Agile approach tends to accept mistakes as not only inevitable, but as a potential source of valuable information.

Create Opportunities

In an environment where exploration leading to a dead end is viewed as an expense to be reduced, true innovation is difficult. However, even in corporate environments where this structure exists, one can avoid this creative damper. Inside engineering departments, engineers, scientists, and developers are often more appreciative of an experimental approach. If the management structure above them occasionally turns a blind eye, exploration can still flourish. In any case, at some level, we have to loosen the reins of pure profitably as a metric around the personnel and departments we hope will be the sources of innovation.

Build Accurate Prototypes

There can also be problems if the modeling or prototyping used as the basis of iteration is incomplete. In 2001, Boeing announced the development of the Sonic Cruiser, a new commercial flying wing that broke the rules of commercial aircraft design. By using a robust modeling approach, Boeing was able to drastically reduce the cost of product development. However, when they built an actual physical mockup of the flying wing and put potential customers in it, the feedback was so appalling that they canned the project. Evidently the sensation of being in a large open cabin with few windows did not sit well with air travelers. If Boeing had considered customer experience earlier in the process, as part of the entire picture, it is unlikely that they would have developed the project at all.

This is all conjecture, but it remains illustrative of a potential pitfall of prototyping. Accurate and appropriately complete prototypes are key to the success or failure of an Agile approach. If the models or prototypes address only a portion of the product, it is possible to overlook critical flaws. However, when the product development process is committed to modeling and frequent testing against reality, the ruler of user experience is more likely to catch these errors early, thus reducing risk. An even more robust approach, such as 3M's actual market test, can also act as a gate to test the product.

Make the Iterative Process Inexpensive and Easy

Another key to promoting success using Agile methods is to reduce the friction of iteration. Friction, in this context, is the cost and effort that goes into each iteration. If you have to build a new manufacturing plant every time you want to prototype the next item in your product line, you're not going to end up building many prototypes. If you can send one of your engineers to the machine shop for an afternoon to do the same thing, your team can go wild exploring different possibilities.

The goal here is to make it easy and cheap to have rapid cycles. In the software world, this is accomplished by having a solid infrastructure, version control, and continuous integration. In hardware engineering, this can mean having a solid grasp of toolsets, limiting the number of development chains across an organization, and implementing actual tools for quick prototyping at various degrees of fidelity. Fortunately, as mentioned early, the tools for this kind of rapid physical prototyping are reaching a tipping point of accessibility and cost. The challenge then becomes keeping up with current possibilities and incorporating them into ongoing product development practices.

Toyota's Product Development method places great emphasis on this part of the process. The personal experience of project personnel can also be leveraged to great effect here. Toyota, by explicitly building teams that are smaller but contain more highly experienced personnel, takes advantage of this. Also, in Toyota's case, approaches that veer away from familiar but expensive solutions and toward innovative but cheaper solutions are heavily encouraged by corporate culture and values. All of these make repetition and exploration easier.

Encourage Open Communication

A final issue that can make or break an Agile approach is communication and collaboration. Agile software development tends to put developers in close physical proximity to enhance communication and collaboration. Sometimes this is possible with product development as well, but often collaboration has to occur across larger departments or even companies. This is where we can reap the benefits of frequent testing and evaluation of prototypes. These frequent build/test cycles allow our disparate teams to communicate through the actual product, alleviating some of our coordination issues with larger groups.

Boeing's digital prototyping process provides some examples of this type of communication. During product development, engineers in one department intentionally trigger conflicts in the digital model with work originating in another department. This conflict initiates specific communication about collaboration, where it is needed. It also allows communication to occur directly between the most appropriate people without requiring messages to jump up and down the corporate structure. If you are in a traditional product development environment, this type of communication might be discouraged as "cheating" or deviating from the official process, raising fears about shortchanging the documentation. However, if you want to encourage an Agile environment, the product itself *is* the documentation, and the only metrics you should care about are effective communication and a working product.

How to Get There

It would be easy to read all this and have several reactions. Discouragement: Our company will never work like that. Disbelief: That would never work for us. Fear: If we did half of this, our company would fall apart or go out of business. These reactions are all valid and there is often a core of truth to them. But, if you look at the history of most companies, their evolution has taken place incrementally, not in giant steps. The path to an internalized, Agile-inspired approach is no different. Setting up a new working team to plan and launch a complete reorganization of the company and its working processes is likely doomed to failure. That's like applying the waterfall approach we are trying to avoid to the problem of our internal processes. A better approach is to apply the Agile iterative, incremental approach to ourselves.

- Take small steps.

- Encourage innovation in a tangible way.

- Provide specific positive feedback and support.

- Decide where you can reduce unneeded documentation.

- Encourage direct communication between disparate working teams.[*]

- Ask yourself what you can do to make your product development more iterative. Do you already do one major release and 10 bug fix releases? You might already be more iterative than you think.

---

[*] Workshops can be helpful as long as you understand the benefits are not the actual exercises or events in the workshops, but rather the fact that all the participants leave, having shared lunch, with each other's phone numbers.

Experiment, Experiment, Experiment

The key point is that companies, like people, are all different. You have to find what will work for your company and for the people who work there. There is not a perfect golden mean; methods are not written in stone. Like the Agile manifesto, these are methods that we have found to be more effective than the alternatives. The advantage of taking small steps to get there is that when these methods start to work, you really know that they are working. It can be hard to believe that you can get by with half the documentation you currently use until you reduce its production a little at a time and then discover that you don't miss it.

So, while the specific methods inspired by an Agile approach are not new or unique, in today's markets they are increasingly appropriate and more likely to lead to success. Prototypes and faster iteration cycles are critical to capturing changing yet relevant information and making errors of the right kind possible. The best product development is as much about discarding the wrong solutions quickly as about finding the right solution. This approach is also a boon for many hardware and software engineers, allowing them room to perform this exploration and further capture the resulting increase in creativity. Finally, with the democratization of some of the development and manufacturing tools, a greater pool of participants will be able to create something new. It allows many of us, in a fundamental way, to make our ideas tangible.

CHAPTER 8

An Uncertain World

"To be uncertain is to be uncomfortable, but to be certain is to be ridiculous."
—Chinese Proverb

"Complex problems have simple, easy to understand, wrong answers."
—Henry Louis Mencken

As we plunge deeper into the 21st century, it's clear that for the foreseeable future things will remain uncertain. This uncertainty pervades the social, cultural, political, and economic aspects of our lives. It's natural to respond to this uncertainty with fear, trepidation, and a desire to put our heads in the sand until things are settled. But will anything ever truly be settled again? It seems a fool's hope. Rather than biding our time, we should adapt to and embrace the uncertainty around us. After all, as Walt Whitman said, "The future is no more uncertain than the present." This uncertainty opens up all manner of new opportunities.

One key opportunity driven by this uncertainty is how the old categories will break down. David Weinberger discusses these trends and their implications in his excellent book, *Everything Is Miscellaneous.*[*] Though the book is ostensibly about the nature of information in a digital world, the forces underlying that miscellany pervade all aspects of society. Google and Yahoo!, once technology companies, are now media players, and their advertising-based business models mean they compete more with Los Angeles and New York than their Silicon Valley brethren. Apple began as a computer company, but has morphed into a consumer electronics company (iPod, iPhone, Apple TV) and the third largest music retailer in the United States, which means its competitors are not only HP, Dell, and Toshiba, but also Sony, Wal-Mart, and Best Buy.

It is this uncertainty and miscellany that renders more traditional approaches to product and service delivery insufficient. You cannot simply analyze your way to success. You cannot optimize your way to profitability. Focusing on risk mitigation allows maverick competitors to surpass you. As markets, people's lives, and the world are becoming more

---

* David Weinberger, *Everything Is Miscellaneous,* (Times Books, 2007)

complex, many of the old, easy answers to business problems are insufficient. Developing creative, agile, and experience-focused approaches will be a key business practice for small and large companies alike.

Just knowing about these approaches isn't enough. To use a phrase from earlier in the book, you need to have a new set of organizational competencies: customer research, design, and agile technological implementation. Customer research allows you to understand and take into account the behaviors and motivations of your customers, and their contexts. It requires you to do away with reductive thinking and get out into their lives and talk to them, then make this newfound understanding of your customers an integral part of your entire organization.

Design allows you to create and sustain a competitive advantage over rivals by taking that understanding of your customer to imagine, create, and deliver great solutions. Design supports an open approach in which anyone in the organization can participate to generate solutions, make insightful and meaningful decisions, and build empathetic services that address needs that customers themselves may not yet know they have. Price and technological advantages are only temporary in most markets, but the ability to continually reframe possibilities and translate new ideas into great experiences is a formula for sustained leadership.

You need agile technological implementation as an organizational competency to quickly prototype your ideas: getting them out of your heads, off your whiteboards, freed from your bullet lists, and out into the world where people can react to them. Working quickly and iteratively helps you understand the way your new product or service works, as well as how feasible it is to manufacture.

These three competencies work in concert to help your organization uncork its potential. Happily, it doesn't cost as much to do this as it did in the past. A small team with little formal research training can produce good research if led by someone with research and facilitation skills. Research methodologies ought to be—and often are—accessible to everyone in your organization. The same is true with design and development. Everyone can and should be involved in creating, prototyping, and evaluating concepts and products, although you'll definitely want to have folks on staff who have the expertise to make designs sing and prototypes move.

As we said before, the uncertainty inherent in the world should be an indication of vast possibilities. We are living and working in a time like no other. It is hardly an exaggeration to say that what we can accomplish is limited only by our imaginations and our ability to truly connect with our customers. The ideas expressed in this book are born from years of experience wrestling with uncertainty. We've been fortunate to work with many excellent organizations, large and small, to help deliver great experiences for their customers. Through our mistakes and successes, we have learned a lot about what it takes to realize possibilities inherent in technologies, markets, and organizations.

The world in which we live and work is subject to change without notice. Succeeding amidst that uncertainty requires continuous improvement. This book is part of that process: we learn more when we share our knowledge with each other. Talking about ideas helps us better understand them; expressing those ideas to others invites them to test our thinking and improve on it. We hope that these ideas will help you improve the work you do designing products and services that provide great experiences. In return, we hope you'll share with us the things you learn along the way.

Bibliography

Books

Berkun, Scott. *The Myths of Innovation.* Sebastopol, California: O'Reilly Media, Inc., 2007.

Brand, Stewart. *How Buildings Learn: What Happens After They're Built.* New York: Penguin, 1995.

Gladwell, Malcolm. *The Tipping Point.* Boston: Little, Brown and Company, 2002

Levy, Steven. *Insanely Great: The Life and Times of Macintosh, the Computer That Changed Everything.* New York: Penguin, 2000.

Locke, Christopher, Rick Levine, Doc Searls, and David Weinberger. *The Cluetrain Manifesto: The End of Business as Usual.* New York: Perseus Books Group, 2001.

Morgan, James, and Jeffrey Liker. *The Toyota Product Development System: Integrating People, Process and Technology.* University Park, Illinois: Productivity Press, 2006.

Norman, Donald. *Emotional Design: Why We Love (or Hate) Everyday Things.* New York: Basic Books, 2005.

Shweder, Richard. *Thinking Through Cultures: Expeditions in Cultural Psychology.* Cambridge: Harvard University Press, 1991.

Weinberger, David. *Everything is Miscellaneous: The Power of the New Digital Disorder.* New York: Times Books, 2007.

Films

Eames, Charles, and Ray Eames, Films of Charles and Ray Eames, Volume 4 (DVD). Image Entertainment, 1967.

Interviews

Davis, Natalia, and Russell Redenbaugh. "Value: Know It, See It, Design For It," interview with Brandon Schauer, The Institute of Design Strategy Conference, 2006.

Adler, Deborah. "A Dose of Design: Target's ClearRX," interview with Brian Collins, BusinessWeek Online, May 9, 2006.

Duncan, Alan K. "Innovation Rigor," interview with Brandon Schauer, The Institute of Design Strategy Conference, 2005.

Fake, Caterina. "MXSF 2007: Interview with Caterina Fake," interview with Peter Merholz, Adaptive Path's Managing Experience Conference, February 12, 2007.

Keeley, Larry. "The Business of NEW," interview with G.K. VanPatter, NextD, 2003.

Veen, Jeffrey, and Khoi Vinh. "Fireside Chat with Khoi Vinh and Jeffrey Veen: 'In-House vs. On Your Own,'" interview with Matt Linderman and Jason Fried, Signal vs. Noise, July 18, 2006.

Jim Wicks. "Weaving Design into Motorola's Fabric," interview with Brandon Schauer, The Institute of Design Strategy Conference, 2006.

Journals and papers

Cooper, Robert G., Scott J. Edgett, and Elko J. Kleinschmidt. "Optimizing the Stage-Gate Process: What Best-Practice Companies are Doing, Part 1." Research Technology Management Volume 45, Number 5, 2002.

Glushko, Robert J., and Lindsay Tabas. "Bridging the 'Front Stage' and 'Back Stage' in Service System Design." School of Information, UC Berkeley, 2007.

Royce, Winston. Managing the Development of Large Software Systems. Proceedings of IEEE WESCON, August 1970, p. 1-09.

Magazines

Bazerman, Max H., and Dolly Chugh. "Decisions Without Blinders." *Harvard Business Review*, January 1, 2006.

Brown, Tim. "Strategy by Design." *Fast Company*, June 2005.

Clark, Hannah. "James Dyson Cleans Up." *Forbes Magazine*, August 1, 2006.

Godin, Seth. "In Praise of the Purple Cow." *Fast Company,* January 2003.

Hackett, James P. "Preparing for the Perfect Product Launch." *Harvard Business Review*, April 2007.

Hargadon, Andrew, and Robert I. Sutton. "Building an Innovation Factory." *Harvard Business Review*, May 1, 2000.

Hindo, Brian. "At 3M, a Struggle Between Efficiency and Creativity." *BusinessWeek*, June 11, 2007.

Jackson, David S. "Palm-to-Palm Combat." *Time Magazine*, March 16, 1998.

Lowry, Tom. "ESPN's Cell-Phone Fumble." *BusinessWeek*, October 30, 2006.

Martin, Roger L. "Creativity That Goes Deep." *BusinessWeek*, August 3, 2005.

Martin, Roger L. "Tough Love." *Fast Company*, October 2006.

McConnon, Aili. "Want a Master of Design with That?" *BusinessWeek*, October 6, 2006.

Meyer, Christopher, and Andre Schwager. "Understanding Customer Experience." *Harvard Business Review*, February 2007.

"The Science of Desire." *BusinessWeek*, June 5, 2006.

Useem, Jerry. "Apple: America's Best Retailer." *Fortune*, March 8, 2007.

Newspapers

"Apple Rises to No. 3 Music Seller in U.S." *Los Angeles Times*, June 22, 2007.

Horovitz, Bruce. "Marketers Take a Close Look At Your Daily Routines." *USA Today*, April 29, 2007.

Online references

Allen, James, Frederick F. Reichheld, Barney Hamilton, and Rob Markey. "Closing the Delivery Gap: How to Achieve True Customer-Led Growth." Bain & Company: Results Brief Newsletter, October 5, 2005.

Ardill, Ralph. "Introduction to Experience Design." Design Council Online, March 26, 2007.

Greenfield, Adam. "On the Ground Running: Lessons From Experience Design." Adobe Design Center's Think Tank, May 16, 2007.

Hemp, Paul. "My Week as a Room-Service Waiter At the Ritz - Customer Service That Puts the 'Ritz' in Ritzy." Harvard Business School: Working Knowledge, July 1, 2002.

Hindo, Brian. "'The Front Lines' of Innovation." BusinessWeek, November 2, 2005.

Kemper, Steve. "Steve Jobs and Jeff Bezos Meet 'Ginger'" Harvard Business School: Working Knowledge, June 16, 2003.

Porter, Michael. "Michael Porter Asks, and Answers: Why Do Good Managers Set Bad Strategies?" Knowledge@Wharton, November 1, 2006.

Porter, Joshua. "The Freedom of Fast Iterations: How Netflix Designs a Winning Web Site." User Interface Engineering, November 14, 2006.

Prescott, Leeann. "Google Calendar Up Threefold Since June." Hitwise Intelligence - Analyst Weblogs, January 3, 2007.

"ClearRX At Target Pharmacy Backgrounder." Target.com. Target Corporation.

Tancer, Bill. "Google, Yahoo! and MSN: Property Size-Up." Hitwise Intelligence - Analyst Weblogs, May 19, 2006.

"Target ClearRX Bottle." Bottom Line Design Awards, 2006.

"Who We Are." Oxo.com. OXO International, 2006.

Presentations

Carbone, Lou. Presentation at Adaptive Path's Managing Experience Conference, February 12, 2007.

Index

A

Acela train service (Amtrak), 99
Adler, Deborah
  design potential, 116–117
  experience strategies, 31–32
  prototyping, 138
Aeron Chair (Herman Miller), 10
aesthetic aspect of design, 9
Agile development models, 157–161
  building prototypes, 167–168
  embedded and networked systems,
    164–166
  experimentation, 171
  guidelines, 170
  iterative approaches, 161–162
    reducing friction of iteration,
      168–169
  Lean Manufacturing, 156–157
  obstacles, 167
  open communication, 169
  use by companies, 162–164
  Waterfall, 154–156
Agile Manifesto, 153–154
*All Marketers Are Liars: The Power of
  Telling Authentic Stories in a
  Low-Trust World,* 46
Altavista search engine, 145
Amazon.com, 109
  API free usage, 147
Amtrak's Acela train service, 99

Apple
  G4 Cube computer, 10
  iPhone
    introduction, 12
    Long "Wow!", 141
  iPhoto software, 91
  iPod
    great ideas, 129
    introduction, 12
    Nike + iPod Sports Kit, 142, 165
    success factors, 83–85
    Touch model, 88
  iTunes, 85–86
    Party Shuffle, 87
    Soundflavor, 130
  iTunes Store, 86–87
    third largest music retailer, 109
  Jobs, Steve, 11–12
    experiential focus, 26
  loyalty programs, 139
  Newton, 33
  optimization practices, 119
  product/service
    development approach, 97–98
    focus, 87–88
  prototyping of retail store, 138
  support of MP3 format, 93
  transitioning into new businesses, 175
artifacts in research, 74–76
ATRAC3 format (Sony), 93
Audrey (3Com), 125

B

Bain and Company, 111
Barnes and Noble superstores, 109
Bellah, Robert, 53
Berkun, Scott, 133
Best Buy, 175
    music retailers, 87
    optimization practices, 119
Blockbuster, 101, 145
Blogger, 91
Blue's Clues (Nickelodeon), 113
Boeing's Sonic Cruiser, 167–168
Bose, 119
BPR (Business Process Reengineering),
        18, 19, 119
Brand, Stewart, 101
brand strategies *versus* experience
        strategies, 29–31
Brown, Tim, 135
Business Process Reengineering. *See* BPR
Business Week
    ethnography, 66
    3M, 107
    Mobile ESPN, 125
    people in research process, 81

C

Calendar
    Google, 27–28
    MSN, 27–28
    Yahoo, 27–28
camera (Eastman Kodak). *See* Kodak
        camera
Carbone, Lou, 29
CarsDirect web site, 137
Castells, Manuel, 50
CD and audiotape players, 83
Center for Bits and Atoms (MIT), 166
Chicago Police Department, 147, 148

ClearRX pill bottles (Target), 31–32
    design potential, 116–117
    prototyping, 138
The Cluetrain Manifesto, 44, 46
CNN.com, 146
Compaq
    internet appliances, 125
competition
    feature matrices, 20
    history, 18–20
    novelty's role, 22–24
    strategies
        parity, 20–22
Consumer Experience Design
        (Motorola), 120
containerization, 3
Cooper, Dr. Robert G., 125
Craigslist, 109
    HousingMaps service, 147
customers
    blending of views, 49–50
    complex relationship with products
            and services, 50–51
    as consumers, 44
    design approaches, 7
    as designers, 146–149
    empathy for, 38, 39–43
    homo economicus, 47–48
    importance to businesses, 43–44
    product development
        behaviors of customers, 55–58
        culture and context, 53–55
        emotion, 51–52
    as sheep, 44–46
    tasks and goals view of, 48–49

D

Darden, 127
Davis, Natalia, 145

Dell Computers, 175
    optimization practices, 119
    supply chain, 18–19
Delta's Song Airlines, 126
design competency
    advantages, 123–131
    failures
        of good execution, 125–126
        of traditional tools, 124–125
    guidelines for success, 127–130
Design for Six Sigma, 124
design process
    as activity, 11
    aspects of, 9–10
    within context of systems and strategy,
        118–119
    decision-making, 114–115
    designing *versus* controlling
        experiences, 144–146
    generative, 113–114
    humanistic, 113
    and ideas, 131–134
        with experience, 135–136
        Long "Wow!", 138–144
        tangible ideas, 137–138
    increasing importance, 8–9
    misconceptions, 115–116
    as organizational competency, 119–120
        competitive competency, 123
        embedding design, 120–123
    potential, 116–117
design research, 62, 72–74
    artifacts, 74–76
    versus market research, 69–70
    personas, 74–76
    prototypes, 76–77
    successful approaches, 83–87
Diamond Rio players, 105
digitization, 3

Disney
    brand strength, 119
    experiences design, 121
Doblin, 124
Duncan, Alan, 122, 123
DVRs
    and TiVo, 13–14
Dyson, James, 134
Dyson vacuum cleaners, 134

E

Eames, Charles, 118
Eastman, George, 81
    camera inventor, 6
Eastman Kodak camera. *See* Kodak
        camera
EasyShare (Kodak), 100
eBay
    API free usage, 147
    Epinions.com, 37
economics *versus* homo economicus,
        47–48
Einstein, Albert, 58
embedded systems in Agile development,
        164–166
emotion
    product development, 51–52
Emotional Design, 51–52
empathy, 38, 39–43
Epinions.com, 37
ethnography, 65–66
evaluative research, 62
Everything is Miscellaneous, 175
*Everyware; The Dawning Age of
        Ubiquitous Computing,* 99
Excite search engine, 145
experience design, 29–31
    new, better, different problems,
        109–111
    obstacles to adoption, 105–107
    systemic coordination, 108–109

experience of customers
  basis of, 17
  ignored, 111–112
  maintaining focus, 26–28
  reasons for importance, 25–26
  TiVo, 13–14
experience strategies, 26
  versus brand strategies, 29–31
  effective strategies, 34
  research requirements, 61–63

F

Fabrication Laboratory (MIT), 166
Fake, Caterina, 131
Fast Company, 81
FedEx, 129
film (roll) for cameras, 6
Flickr, 37, 91–94
  About page, 131
Forbes, 81
Forth and Town stores (Gap, Inc.), 126
Friendster, 37

G

G4 Cube computer (Apple), 10
Gap Inc.'s Forth and Town stores, 126
Garrett, Jesse James, 27
Gateway, 125
General Mills, 54
generative research, 62
Gladwell, Malcom, 113
Global Design Centers (Samsung), 72–73
globalization, 3
Gmail (Google), 27
Godin, Seth, 46
Good Grips Angled Measuring Cup
    (OXO and Smart Design), 139–141,
    142

Google
  API free usage, 147
  designing in real time, 135
  experience *versus* brand strategies, 31
  versus previous search engines, 145
  transitioning into new businesses, 175
Google Calendar, 27–28
Google Gmail, 27
Google Maps, 147
Greenfield, Adam, 99

H

Habits of the Heart, 53
Hackett, Jim, 127
Harley-Davidson, 139
Harvard Business Review, 127
Hawkins, Jeff, 33
Herman Miller's Aeron Chair, 10
Hewlett-Packard. *See* HP
homo economicus, 47–48
Hotbot search engine, 145
Hotmail (MSN), 27
House, Chuck, 162
HousingMaps service (Craigslist), 147
How Buildings Learn, 101
HP (Hewlett-Packard), 118, 175
  iterative approaches, 162
  optimization practices, 119
  oscilloscope design, 162
Huggies products (Kimberly-Clark), 54,
    55

I

IBM, Trident submarine systems, 161
idea lab (Adaptive Path), 131–133
IdeaLab!, 137
IDEO, 135
  design of Acela train service, 99
  people in research process, 81
  SPARC program, 122

Intel
  internet appliances, 125
  People and Practices group, 72–73
  people in research process, 81
Interactive Marketing Group, 97
iPhone (Apple)
  introduction, 12
  Long "Wow!", 141
iPhoto software, 91
iPod (Apple)
  expanding product functionality, 87–88
  great ideas, 129
  introduction, 12
  product/service focus, 87–88
  success factors, 83–85
  Touch, 88
iterative development approaches,
  161–162
  reducing friction of iteration, 168–169
iTunes (Apple)
  Party Shuffle, 87
  Soundflavor, 130
iTunes Store (Apple), 86–87
  third largest music retailer, 109

J

Johnson, Kelly, 166

K

Kairos, Inc., 145
Kimberly-Clark's Huggies products, 54,
  55
Kodak camera
  digital photography, 100
  EasyShare cameras, 100
  ongoing relationships with customers,
  81–83
  "photographic apparatus," 4–7

L

Lean Manufacturing development
  models (Toyota), 156–157, 163
Liedtka, Jeanne, 127
Lockheed's Skunk Works, 162, 166
Lowry, Tom, 125
Lucente, Sam, 118–119

M

Mail (Yahoo), 27
"Managing the Development of Large
  Software Systems," 155
Maps (Google), 147
market research, 62
  versus design research, 69–70
Martin, Roger, 120
Mayo Clinic's SPARC program, 121–123,
  143
McDonald's Corporation
  explorative design, 114–115
  top-down organization, 146
McLuhan, Marshall, 69–70
Mercury systems software, 161
Michalski, Jerry, 44
Microsoft
  internet appliances, 125
  people in research process, 81
  research of customers and use of
    products, 54
  Zune, 88
MIT's Fab Lab, 166
Mobile ESPN, 125–126
Moore's Law, 8
Motorola's Consumer Experience Design,
  120
MP3 players
  early options, 83, 84
  evolving into media players, 85
  support by Apple, 93

MSN Calendar, 27–28
MSN Hotmail, 27
Museum of Modern Art (New York), 10
MySpace, 37
The Myths of Innovation, 133

N

NASA's X-15 project, 161
Netflix, 101, 145
    great ideas, 129
    testing ideas, 133
NetPromoter Score, 138
networked systems in Agile development,
    164–166
Nickelodeon's *Blue's Clues,* 113
Nike
    loyalty programs, 139
    Nike + iPod Sports Kit, 142, 165
Norman, Don, 51
novelty in competition, 22–24
NW-HD1 player (Sony), 93

O

Ofoto, 90
Old Spice High Endurance Hair & Body
    Wash product (Proctor & Gamble),
    50–51
One Laptop Per Child, 129
On-The-Go application
    (WeightWatchers), 143–144
OXO's Good Grips Angled Measuring
    Cup, 139–141, 142

P

Packard, David, 162
PalmPilot, 33
Party Shuffle, Apple's iTunes, 87
People and Practices group (Intel), 72–73
personas in research, 74–76
Phaeton (Volkswagen), 126

Photos (Yahoo!), 84, 90
Picasa software, 91
PJB-100 MP3 player, 84
Post-It notes (3M), 106–107
Proctor & Gamble
    Old Spice High Endurance Hair &
        Body Wash product, 50–51
    research of customers and use of
        products, 54
Product Development method (Toyota),
    169
product/service development
    and customers
        behaviors of customers, 55–58
        complex relationship, 50–51
        emotion factor, 51–52
    cycles, 3
    feature-based, 8
    standalone, 3
    tactics
        coordinated or chaotic, 97–98
        online successes, 90–94
        over-engineering, 98–99, 101
        services behaving like products,
            94–96
        successful, 83–88
        unsuccessful, 88–90
    technologies and features copied,
        12–13
prototypes in research, 76–77, 137–138
Puma's Mongolian Shoe BBQ, 148

Q

qualitative *versus* quantitative research,
    63–65, 66
    mixing methods, 71–72

R

Rademacher, Paul, 147
ReplayTV, 14
reports in research, 68–69

research
    design process integration, 72–74
        artifacts, 74–76
        personas, 74–76
        prototypes, 76–77
    ethnography, 65–66
    ineffective tactics, 67–70
    market *versus* design research, 69–70
    organizational competency, 70–71
    quantitative *versus* qualitative research,
        63–65, 66
        mixing methods, 71–72
    requirements for product/service
        development, 61–63
The Rise of the Network Society, 50
ROI (return on investment), 47
Rotman School of Management, 120
Royce, Winston, 155

S

SafeRX pill bottles
    design potential, 116–117
    experience strategies, 31–32
    prototyping, 138
Samsung's Global Design Centers, 72–73
Scientific American, 4
Scripps Networks HGTV.com, 75
Seattle Public Library, 29
Segway scooters, 23–24
services, developing. *See* product/service
    development
Sesame Street, 113
Shutterfly, 90
Six Sigma, 18, 119
Skunk Works (Lockheed), 162, 166
Smart Design (with OXO) Good Grips
    Angled Measuring Cup, 140
social software, 37
software development approaches,
    153–154

Song Airlines, 126
Sonic Cruiser (Boeing), 167–168
Sony, 175
    ATRAC3 format, 93
    product/service development
        approach, 97–98
    Walkman, 83
Soundflavor, 130
SPARC program (Mayo Clinic), 121–123,
    143
SR-71 Blackbird (Lockheed's Skunk
    Works), 162
Star Gate, 124, 125
Starbucks, 21
Steelcase, 127
Steve Jobs
    Apple's CEO, 11–12
    experiential focus, 26
Supply Chain Management, 119
sympathy *versus* empathy, 39

T

Taco Bell, 21
Target's ClearRX pill bottles
    design potential, 116–117
    experience strategies, 31–32
    optimization practices, 119
    prototyping, 138
tasks and goals view of customers, 48–49
Taylor, Edward, 18
Threadless online t-shirt store, 148
3Com's Audrey, 125
3M
    iterative approach, 163
    Post-It notes and masking tape,
        106–107
time and motion studies, 18
The Tipping Point, 113

TiVo
    versus DVRs, 13–14
    experience *versus* brand strategies, 31
    great ideas, 129
    versus VCRs, 165
Toshiba, 175
Total Quality Management, 119
Touch model, iPod (Apple), 88
Toyota
    Lean Manufacturing development
        models, 156–157, 163
    Product Development method, 169
Trident submarine systems (IBM), 161
Typepad, 91

U

U-2 (Lockheed's Skunk Works), 162
UK Design Council
    experience design, 29–31
United States Holocaust Memorial
    Museum, 29
USA Today
    customers and context of using
        products, 54
usability practices
    Epinions.com, 37
user research, 62

V

VCRs *versus* DVRs and TiVo, 13–14, 165
Veen, Jeffrey, 135
Volkswagen's Phaeton, 126

W

Walkman (Sony), 83
Wal-Mart, 175
    music retailers, 87
    optimization practices, 119
    supply chain, 119
Waterfall development models, 154–156
WeightWatchers' On-The-Go application,
    143–144
Weinberger, David, 175
Wicks, Jim, 120
Wi-Fi connectivity, 88
Wilkens, Todd, 69
WordPress, 91

Y

Yahoo!, 175
Yahoo Calendar, 27–28
Yahoo Mail, 27
Yahoo! Photos, 84, 90
YouTube, 88, 146

Z

Zune (Microsoft), 88

The O'Reilly Advantage

Stay Current and Save Money

Order books online:
www.oreilly.com/order_new

Questions about our
products or your order:
order@oreilly.com

Join our email lists: Sign up
to get topic specific email
announcements or new
books, conferences, special
offers and technology news
elists@oreilly.com

For book content
technical questions:
booktech@oreilly.com

To submit new book
proposals to our editors:
proposals@oreilly.com

Contact us:
O'Reilly Media, Inc.
1005 Gravenstein Highway N.
Sebastopol, CA U.S.A. 95472
707-827-7000 or
800-998-9938
www.oreilly.com

Did you know that if you register
your O'Reilly books, you'll get
automatic notification and upgrade
discounts on new editions?

**And that's not all! Once you've registered
your books you can:**

» Win free books, T-shirts and O'Reilly Gear

» Get special offers available only to registered
O'Reilly customers

» Get free catalogs announcing all our new
titles (US and UK Only)

**Registering is easy! Just go to
www.oreilly.com/go/register**

Try the online edition free for 45 days

Get the information you need when you need it, with Safari Books Online. Safari Books Online contains the complete version of the print book in your hands plus thousands of titles from the best technical publishers, with sample code ready to cut and paste into your applications.

Safari is designed for people in a hurry to get the answers they need so they can get the job done. You can find what you need in the morning, and put it to work in the afternoon. As simple as cut, paste, and program.

To try out Safari and the online edition of the Subject To Change: Creating Great Products & Services for an Uncertain World FREE for 45 days, go to www.oreilly.com/go/safarienabled and enter the coupon code ZOZFJGA.

To see the complete Safari Library visit:
safari.oreilly.com